Quick & Kosher

Recipes From *The Bride Who Knew Nothing*

by Jamie Geller

FELDHEIM
JERUSALEM · NEW YORK

Quick & Kosher
Recipes From *The Bride Who Knew Nothing*
by Jamie Geller

Photography *Jerry Errico*, Book Design *Alessandro/Weber Design*, Calligraphy *Gina Jonas*, Food Styling *Brian Preston-Campbell*, Prop Styling *Kristen Palmer, Lisa Schaffler*, Content Editing and Additional Writing *Charlotte Friedland*, Recipe Consultant *Joy Lynn Devor*, Recipe Testing *Joy Lynn Devor, Brian Preston-Campbell, Laurie Knoop, Alice Piacenza*, Recipe Editing *Sylvia Carter*, Recipe Coordinating *Karen Geller-Hittleman*, Copy Editing *Judith H. Bernstein*, Proofreading *Elissa Epstein*, Publisher *Feldheim Publishers*

FELDHEIM PUBLISHERS
JERUSALEM - NEW YORK
Copyright © 2007 by Feldheim Publishers and Jamie Geller
Photographs copyright © 2007 by Jerry Errico

FELDHEIM PUBLISHERS
POB 43163, Jerusalem, Israel 91431
208 Airport Executive Park, Nanuet, NY 10954
www.feldheim.com
www.quickandkosher.com

Library of Congress Cataloging – in – Publication Data

Geller, Jamie.
Quick & Kosher: Recipes From *The Bride Who Knew Nothing* / Jamie Geller.
p. cm.
Includes index
ISBN 978-1-58330-960-5
1. Jewish cookery. I. Title.
TX724.G45 2008
641.5'676–dc22   2007019432

Printed in Israel

10   9   8   7   6   5   4   3   2   1

This book is dedicated in loving memory of my grandmothers and my husband's
father and grandfather:

Miriam bas Gershon
Miriam Zuckerman

Golda bas Chaim Hersh
Aranka Mendelovici

Yaakov Leib ben Shaul
Jack Lewis Geller

Shaul ben Zev
Saul Geller

They impact our lives every day, as we never forget them and never stop talking
about them. We learned and still continue to learn so much from them: cooking
techniques, of course, but more importantly, how to be a mensch. We are so grateful
to be able to put their names in print and remember them in this manner.

What's Inside…

Confessions of a Jewish Bride

You might call this the *I Didn't Tell Him I Couldn't Cook Cookbook*. Back when I met my future husband, I was a dedicated, 24/7, fast-track producer at a major cable network. I was always on the move, traveling all over the country and overseas, interviewing actors and musicians who are better known than most world leaders. That was my life and kitchens were not a part of it. But before I had a chance to reveal that I had been raised on takeout and cooking was totally off my radar, we were engaged to be married.

Even before meeting Hubby, I had made a commitment to myself to become a more observant Jew (known in Hebrew as a *baalas teshuvah*, abbreviated in hip-Hebrew to "*BT*"). If you think that decision has nothing to do with cooking, as I did, get ready for the news: There are a zillion and one Jewish occasions for which you'll be expected to produce lavish dinners for a zillion and one people. The bottom line is that whether you're religiously observant or not, kosher or not, chances are you celebrate everything with food.

To say I had a lot to learn is the understatement of the century. Truth be told, when it comes to homemaking, I had always been at a loss. I had never threaded a needle or sewed on a button, never kicked open an ironing board, done my own laundry or folded a shirt. When we got married, I was too embarrassed to suggest to my husband that we send our socks and towels to the dry cleaners. So I learned my way around the washing machine, figured out how to turn on the dryer and Tide became my new best friend.

I know what you're thinking. Why didn't her mother teach her those basics? Was she raised by servants?

Let me put your mind at ease. My mother is a great mom, but not someone you'd crown as the *Supreme Balabusta*. She was born in Transylvania in Romania and moved here with her family as a teenager. Coming from a strong European culture, she hit America with a twinkle of hope in her eye and a spring in her step, embracing all the wonderfully American opportunities available to women. It was exhilarating to see that women could have jobs outside the kitchen. So she left it, never to return.

The irony is that she could have studied the culinary arts under the wings of my grandparents, two gourmet chefs who owned restaurants in the suburbs of Philly. My grandfather, who is now 86, still occasionally throws on his white chef's apron to create magical dishes. I think he talks to his soup, coaxing the herbs to bring out their flavors. Years later, and miles away in New York, I can still smell those full-bodied aromas.

Maybe Mom needed her own space; maybe she just detested kitchen chores. It's not for me to judge. But the result is that cooking skipped a generation, and almost skipped two.

Fortunately, when Hubby found me out, he generously dismissed the fact that I had married him without divulging that I knew zero about food prep. He cheerfully helped me learn the most extraordinary things, like how to sift flour, how to pluck a chicken, how to choose a melon. Amazing!

Little by little, I learned what every homemaker knows and maybe more, because I insisted that recipes had to be quick and really, really easy. Today, I'm literally cookin' on all four burners. My mother is flabbergasted when she sees me in the kitchen cooking up a storm, testing recipes, planning parties – and without calling a caterer.

But I'm not pretentious about my new-found skills. I know that this cookbook of 15-minute prep recipes would be sacrilegious to my grandparents. My grandmother probably went fishing herself for the carp, or whatever fish you use, for her famous gefilte fish. She and my grandfather were serious bakers, too. They used to create a 12-layer Hungarian Dobos torte for our birthdays. Each incredible layer was baked separately in the oven and smothered in homemade chocolate cream, with a deliciously thick coating of caramelized sugar on top. That's Hungarian cooking for you – four days to make, four minutes to eat.

After reading the above confessions, you'd think that I entirely missed out on Old World kitchen secrets. Surprisingly, both of my parents taught me a thing or two that I will joyfully pass on to you.

This book, then, is an unexpected ode to my parents and to my grandparents for everything I learned and didn't learn from them. Taste buds never go out of fashion, but they can be updated. While my grandparents may have simmered their scrumptious delicacies for hours on end, today's clueless-in-the-kitchen generation is happy to whip up an appealing and yummy meal in minutes.

So get yourself into that kitchen! I'll help you along, teaching you all the things I sweated over when I was starting out. I found that it's not hard to create a wonderful family dining experience. You'll find that learning to prepare a new dish takes on an excitement all its own. Just remember to garnish it with love.

Setting Up Your Kitchen

Everyone makes a big deal about housewares and bridal registries. As a bride-to-be, I didn't understand what all the fuss was about. I asked my future mother-in-law, Karen, "Why register? What do I need?" She was stunned, but gracious. "What do you need? Why, you have to set up your kitchen," she said sweetly.

She calmly explained that I would want to select gifts for the shower, useful gifts like Tupperware and mixers. Now, don't get me wrong – I have never been one to turn down a present. But I like cold, hard cash, clothes or California plane tix. I'll take gift certificates to any spa anywhere, but beaters and bakeware?

But, like a good daughter-in-law-to-be, I wound up trailing after my fiancé's mother down the aisles of a classy housewares superstore. (Who knew?) She happens to be an awesome mother-in-law and we did end up bonding and having a wonderful time, but the experience made my head spin. Shelves piled from floor to ceiling with kitchen tchotchkes surrounded me. All the gizmos and gadgets and blenders and bowls looked lovely in their displays, but in my house? What on earth would I do with them?

As I followed her around in a daze, hopelessly fishing in my bag for a pen and old receipts I could scribble notes on, Karen marched briskly down every aisle, consulting a pre-printed checklist of what we would need. She'd cheerfully point out items and then enter them in a color-coded binder she'd brought along just for that purpose. I had to be reminded that I needed two sets of everything – one for dairy and one for meat – for my kosher kitchen. Maybe this should have been obvious to me, but up to that point, paper goods had been my china of choice. Back then, as a single girl living in Manhattan, I was using my oven for storage. My idea of dinner was a salad with whatever takeout leftovers were in the fridge.

The highlight of our tour was the food processor section. The cool colors caught my eye before the actual appliances did. As I was contemplating getting the candy apple red one, strictly from a décor point of view, my mother-in-law was going on and on about the many uses of this 15-pound wonder.

She tactfully mentioned that it is my sister-in-law Chanie's favorite food toy. She even uses it to make all natural baby food for her triplets! Of course!

I thought to myself, "I just met this woman. I don't want to insult her. I'll never need this thing. I can always exchange it."

So I dutifully put "processor thingy" on my registry list, deciding to go with the streamlined black one, since black is a thinning color.

The food processor arrived a couple of days later, compliments of my mom's best buddies. The box was heavy and filled with strange attachments, but the kicker was that this crazy contraption came with an instructional video. "If I don't have time to watch my exercise videos," I muttered to myself, "you can be sure I won't be popping this in any time soon." That was then.

Now I love that sweet little machine. I use it all the time, even if it's just for one dish. Did I say love? Because I do mean love. It's such a time saver, especially for potato kugel. Who grates by hand anymore? If you are one of those people who think that the secret to a light and fluffy potato kugel is in the blood and sweat, toil and tears of hand-grating the potatoes, I promise you you're mistaken. People ask me for my recipe all the time and I never hand grate! I truly believe G-d created food processors just for people like me.

But I have no interest in other gadgets. I own no special equipment – no torches, no spring-form pans, no immersion blenders. Gotcha. I never heard of an immersion blender either until Joy, this book's recipe tester, asked if she would need to buy a dairy one for this project. To this day, I don't own one and don't plan to!

I have an aversion to scales, too – and not just the one in the kitchen. I know a seasoned chef (Joy's mother) who uses a kitchen scale to weigh each of her meatballs to make sure they are exactly the same size. You won't catch me using one. But Joy's mom turned me on to the mini food processor, which is perfect for dicing one onion or a few cloves of garlic. It makes me feel great to know that real chefs use time-savers, too!

Pictures are the best part of most cookbooks, and the only part I used to understand. You've probably looked at pictures that made you want to run out and buy everything you'd need for that mouth-watering recipe. Until you discovered that you'd have to shop for weeks in specialty stores, not just to find the ingredients, but the equipment, too. Forget it.

Here are my simple lists of "must haves," whether you need directions to the oven or you know your way around the kitchen with your eyes closed, but could still use a few shortcuts. Don't get nervous. This is basic stuff you can find in your supermarket and local stores.

EQUIPMENT

A Great Set of Knives

If it seems macabre to you to stock up on these lethal-looking implements, get over it. Use the right knife, and you'll find yourself cutting not only foods, but the time it takes to get them to your table.

There are many kinds of knives, but the essentials are:

> Chef's knife (8-inch)
>
> Utility (all purpose) knife
>
> Serrated (bread) knife
>
> Paring knife
>
> Carving (slicing) knife w/ 6-inch fork

A Good Cutting Board

Wood and plastic are best. If you're like me and hand washing is not in your repertoire, go for plastic.

Measuring Cups and Spoons

Seems so obvious, but my first year of marriage I used a mug and a soupspoon as benchmarks. Cups should be see-through glass or plastic with handles and pour spouts. Splurge on two sets of spoons so you don't have to re-wash in the middle of food prep.

Many, Many, Many Bowls

You really can never have too many. You'll need large ones, small ones and everything in between. Nesting bowls provide streamlined storage.

Food Processor

Perfect for everything from blending dressings to grating potatoes for a kugel that serves 16. A mini processor is terrific for small jobs, like dicing one or two onions (without crying), but if you can only invest in one go for the biggie.

Hand or Stand Mixer

Unless you are a serious baker (a one-woman-bake-sale kind of gal) a good hand mixer will take care of all your blending tasks, and it'll fit in a drawer. A stand mixer is much more expensive, but it can handle heavy-duty or higher quantity mixing needs, with the added convenience of keeping your hands free.

Glass and Ceramic Bakeware

Baking and serving in one dish is quick and convenient. These cooking and serving pieces are attractive, versatile and easy to clean, too.

A Family Heirloom Pan

A cooking utensil that has stood the test of time and is known to bake a certain dish just right. I cannot bake the famous Geller challah kugel without my father-in-law's grease stained old pan. I'm sure that pan brings me mazel: challah kugel was one of the first dishes I got right. If you're not in possession of an ancestral pan, it's up to you to create one for future generations!

Disposable Baking Pans

These pans bake well and make clean-up a cinch. But be careful: baking usually takes more time in disposables, and using them exclusively is going to cost you.

Roasting Pan

A 12 x 17-inch pan is best, but measure your oven before buying. Go with a pan that has a good heft, secure, comfortable handles, and a bit of a flare on the rim.

Deep Fry and Instant-read Digital Thermometers

End the guesstimating game. (Is it done yet?) These handy tools will tell you when your oil is that perfect temperature, and when your meat is good to go.

Skillets (a.k.a Sauté and Frying Pans)

To get started, you'll want to have a 12- or 14-inch *large* skillet and a 10-inch *medium* one. It's helpful to have lids, too.

Slow Cooker

The ultimate quickie cook's cooker. Dump in the ingredients and let it do all the work for you, while you do whatever it is that you do out of the kitchen.

Soup Pot (Stockpot)

A *must*, and not just for soups. Think pasta, pot roasts, meatballs and stews. These come in a full range of sizes, but a 6-quart soup pot is an all purpose basic.

Sauce Pan

A dish without sauce is like a salad without dressing. I'm an "extra sauce please" gal, so I need a few of these. If you buy only one, a 2- to 3-quart pan is the way to go. But if you're buying several, a 1- to 2-quart sauce pan is also very handy.

Ramekins

A ramekin gives an authentic look to all your French dishes and its heatproof quality lets you take it from the broiler or oven straight to the table. Voilà!

Bundt Pan

A fluted Bundt pan makes any cake look and taste impressive, even if you made it from a mix! No wonder it's the top-selling cake pan in the world!

Aluminum Cookie Sheet

Incredibly useful for things like jelly rolls, cookies and individual pizzas. A non-stick coating will make baked goods easy to remove, or line your sheet with parchment paper.

Pastry Brush

Regretfully, no one ever encouraged my inner artist. Now, with this little brush, I can flex my artistic muscle as I paint beaten egg over my challahs and deli rolls.

Whisk

You wouldn't believe how many kinds of whisks are out there: balloon whisks, French whisks, birch whisks, coil whisks and the indispensable Ten-Point Aquatic Quadratic Neon Whisk (just kidding). I say keep it simple. I use a basic wire whisk for beating eggs and whisking together dressings.

Peeler

My grandmother could peel an apple with a knife in one elegant, circular motion. Not me. I need a peeler. One with a nice, sharp blade.

Sealable Plastic Bags

They come in sizes ranging from snack packs to 2 gallons and have innumerable uses, such as marinating your meat, storing cut vegetables, even dressing a salad.

Kitchen Timer and Eraser Board

When you're preparing five different dishes at once, the timer and eraser board will help you keep track of cooking times – and your sanity.

Your Hands

A real chef's best tool is his or her hands. Good chefs (I'm told) get down and dirty, mixing and kneading with their bare hands. Just make sure yours are super duper clean!

SPICES

Salt: Kosher Salt, Sea Salt and Table Salt

Kosher and Sea are both coarse-flake salts, but they taste different because the latter contains trace amounts of minerals from evaporated sea water. Table is fine grain salt and, since it dissolves quicker than its coarse cousins, it should be your salt of choice when baking.

Coarse Black Pepper

It has so much more flavor than regular ground pepper. Don't be afraid to use it.

Dried Parsley Flakes

This stuff is fantastic for taste and presentation. Crush the flakes in your hand to bring out more flavor.

Garlic Powder and Onion Powder

They count as one since they are almost always used together. In a pinch, I've substituted one for the other and my unknowing victims – I mean guests – were none the wiser.

Paprika

Whether you call it "papreeka" or paaprika," it's the red spice that imparts such a pretty color. The remedy for pale roasted chicken, it adds a flavor all its own, too.

Cinnamon and Nutmeg

Another fab spice duo. Their aroma will give your kitchen a warm, homey smell.

Rosemary or Thyme

Choose a favorite and make it your specialty spice. Do you know that old folk song, "Scarborough Fair?" Until I started cooking, I thought the sage was an old man, rosemary a girl's name, thyme – well, time – and I always wondered what they all had to do with parsley.

Curry, Cumin and Cayenne Pepper

These are spices we don't use a lot in traditional Eastern European Jewish cooking, but I learned to love them thanks to the exotic cooking of my friend Monet. (Yes, that's her real name.)

PANTRY ITEMS

You can always whip up a satisfying salad if you have these items at arm's length:

White Shoepeg and Sweet Yellow Corn Niblets
Hearts Of Palm
Black Beans
Chickpeas
Canned Tuna
Craisins
Canned Tomatoes, Tomato Sauce and Marinara Sauce

These all impart huge amounts of flavor and are fabulous time savers.

Osem Soup Mix

(chicken, beef, onion, vegetable and consommé)

The secret seasoning every quickie chef needs in order to add flavor, not just to soups, but also to meat, chicken and sides.

Non-stick Cooking Spray and Baking Spray

For cooking or baking almost anything. If there's the tiniest threat that your culinary masterpiece will be sticky, just spray this on the pan and stop worrying!

FRIDGE, FREEZER AND VEGGIE BIN STAPLES

Salad Basics

Always have these essentials in stock: Your favorite lettuce, carrots, cucumbers and tomatoes. Go with minis or smaller varieties when available. You'll pare down your cutting time and can also grab them for snacks on the go.

Onions

Yellow, Spanish, Vidalia and red provide lots of variety. Sometimes you need a little sweetness, sometimes a little color and sometimes you just need an onion.

Bell Peppers

You can get these in red, green, yellow and orange. The colors bring life to your everyday recipes, with added flavor, too.

Celery

Standard in soups, celery adds a delicious, surprising crunch to salads.

Avocado

Guacamole is always a crowd-pleaser. And a ripe avocado spread on a piece of bread with a dash of kosher salt can pass for a meal – at least for girls like me who are allergic to stoves.

Potatoes

Keep good old Idaho potatoes and a few yams around always. For specialty dishes and occasions, splurge on novelty potatoes like baby red bliss and fingerling.

Frozen Fruit

Strawberries, blueberries, raspberries and peaches are great for desserts, fruit soups and smoothies!

Honeydew and Cantaloupe

Keeping one or both in the house provides a

quick way to whip up an appealing fruit salad. Using a melon ball thingy always makes for an attractive presentation. (It's all in the wrist.)

Frozen Puff Pastry Sheets
For everything from deli rolls to cookies. Just having these around stimulates cooking creativity.

Frozen Crushed Garlic Cubes and Jarred Crushed Garlic
These save you the time spent peeling and dicing garlic and prevent you from reeking of garlic for the rest of the day. Check packaging for fresh equivalents.

Hagafen Red Wine
Under no circumstances should you use cooking wine as it is full of excessive salt and other unnecessary flavors, which will just throw off your spices. It's always a nice idea to use the same wine you plan on serving with the meal when preparing the dish.

CONDIMENTS

Olive Oil and Canola Oil
Although it's expensive, I used to use olive oil exclusively as a dressing and for cooking. (Maybe that's why my bank account was always so low. Too much olive oil. Or was it too many shoes?) When it is not essential to a recipe, canola is another good choice.

Balsamic, Red Wine and White Vinegar
Vinegars galore! Each kind has its own time and place. Substitutions rarely work because they have such deliciously distinctive tastes.

Soy Sauce and Teriyaki Sauce
They're not just for Asian food! Soy has a strong, salty taste and can be used in a myriad of recipes to give them a special

tang. You can throw teriyaki sauce on anything and nonchalantly tell inquiring minds, "Oh this? It's just a teriyaki glaze." Sounds impressive, doesn't it?

Toasted Sesame, Hot Pepper Sesame and Plain Ol' Sesame Oil
Trust me, there is nothing plain about these oils. They're expensive, but they impart a delicious aroma and taste to many specialty dishes.

Lemon Juice
Fresh-squeezed lemons are best, but who has the time? Keep a bottle of prepared lemon juice around for dressings, sauces and marinades.

Grated Parmesan Cheese
It lends a tasty touch to most dairy dishes with the added bonus of lasting in the fridge forever.

Mustard, Ketchup and Mayonnaise
Dijon- and honey Dijon-style mustards are delicious ingredients in dips, sauces, marinades and dressings, and you can't be American without keeping the classic yellow kind and ketchup in the fridge. Even my European-born family has adopted this practice. As for mayo, I prefer the "light" variety. I don't cut calories in many places, but this is an easy place to do it.

Secrets of the 15-Minute Chef

TIME SAVERS

Plan, Plan, Plan

It sounds so basic, but you'd be surprised how many people don't bother to plan ahead. Back in the old days, I would actually start preparing a new recipe, only to realize about halfway through that I didn't have all the ingredients.

Now I like to invest a little time each day preparing for Shabbos, which is the focal point of my family's week. This same process works for any entertaining occasion.

Day 1:   I plan the menu, writing down the ingredients I'll need for each dish.
Day 2:   I make up a shopping list, including staples we buy every week.
Day 3:   I shop.
Day 4:   I go back for the stuff I forgot to put on my list.
Day 5:   I cook and bake.
Day 6:   I set the table and reheat everything I planned for the Friday night meal. Then I light the candles and relax in their warm glow. The food smells delicious. My guests are on their way. And I'm ready.

Frozen Is Your Friend

If you're short on time, remember that a frozen or jarred novelty item presented beautifully can draw as many compliments as your own specialties. The fact that it isn't homemade will probably fly right under your guests' radar.

Be a Cubist

Use pre-cubed meat for shish kabob, chunked beef for stews and pre-sliced pepper steak. Other time savers – like pre-skinned and cubed butternut squash – are hiding in the produce department, just waiting for you to discover them.

Leave Some Things to the Experts

Don't fillet or skin fish yourself; have it done at the store, instead. Turkey wings are notoriously difficult to split, but your butcher can do them in a jiffy. If you ask nicely, he may even take care of your chicken wings. And while trying to hack at spaghetti squash will leave you breathless, your produce guy can easily slice it in half. These pros will do a better job in a fraction of the time. Let 'em!

Bag It

Wash and inspect all your vegetables for bugs,* then cut and bag them ahead of time. Better yet, eliminate cutting altogether and buy whatever you can find in mini: think fingerling potatoes, baby bell peppers and finger fruits. Packages of pre-washed and shredded carrots, cabbage and coleslaw mixes are all the rage now, too. They're ready to eat or mix into your dishes and salads. Have you ever heard of anything better?

Substitute Dried For Fresh

Cooking with fresh ingredients is nice, but it takes more time. People will still love your

---

Jewish law does not permit the consumption of insects, and requires that all produce be checked. Consult a rabbi for recommended procedures.

cooking if you rely on dried herbs. As a rule of thumb, when substituting the more potent dried herbs for their fresh counterparts, cut the measurement in half.

Use Instant Hot Water
Waiting for water to boil is like watching paint dry. Using instant hot water from your kitchen water cooler or from one of those instant hot water faucets installed in your sink is a huge time saver.

TIPS YOUR MOTHER NEVER TOLD YOU

Turn Off The Smoke Alarm
During my first year of marriage, I would sometimes work late, come home, start cooking for Shabbos and set off the smoke alarm – usually around 2 a.m. I had visions of my poor neighbors rolling their eyes, punching their pillows and muttering, "There goes that new bride, *trying* to cook again." So, turn off your smoke alarm if you cook late at night. And please make sure to turn it right back on when you're finished.

Know Your Oven
The knob on my first stove was almost 30 degrees off, *obviously* the reason my dinners were either undercooked or burnt to a crisp. Buy one of those handy oven temperature gauges so you can find out what the knob is not telling you.

Test Meals
Before you have your in-laws or your husband's boss over, pre-test your dishes on anyone who's willing to live dangerously. I neglected to run try-outs and … well, I won't give you the sordid details.

Don't Be Afraid To Delegate
When guests ask if they can bring something, say "sure." Most people have go-to recipes they can offer. And they'll love knowing that they contributed to the success of the meal.

Leave Your Pride At The Kitchen Door
When you have questions or need advice, just ask! One time, I called Judy, my stepmother-in-law, while she was at the hairdresser, forcing her to shout over the dryers about "the secret to a light meatball."

Organize Yourself
Learn from my experience: Always read the recipe and prepare your

ingredients and equipment. Once you've washed the chicken is no time to run to the store or go searching for a pan at the back of your cabinet.

ENTERTAINING TRICKS

Know Your Guests
Inquire about food allergies or diet restrictions *before* you even plan your meal. There's nothing more awkward than bringing a fabulous roast to the table and finding out your guest is a vegetarian. It forces you to scramble back to the kitchen (ever so gracefully) to frantically hunt up something – granola bars? – that you can serve instead.

Be Ready For Kids
Have a few specialty items up your sleeve, even if they're store-bought. Chicken nuggets and ketchup are popular for the main course and sprinkled cupcakes or ices for dessert are always a hit. Happy kids equal happy parents!

The Power of Hors D'Oeuvres
When you bring out a tray of these little appetizers before the meal, you not only relax your guests, you show that you are a relaxed hostess with not a care in the world. Everyone will come to the table primed for a pleasant time.

Set A Striking Table
Even before the food comes out, you're preparing your guests for a dining experience. An attractive table setting doesn't have to be expensive, though. Go for the unbreakable stuff. It often comes in great colors and bold patterns, so you can make a statement without risking your bank account or your good china.

Presentation, Presentation, Presentation

Presentation is a fabulous way to psych-out the palate, and if you're a chef-in-training, it will buy you some time. When my best friend Rozanna first came to our house for dinner, she thought my mother was the most superb cook on the planet. It wasn't till almost a year later that she discovered the entire meal was takeout, placed onto our own dishes. See, Mom follows a hard and fast rule in entertaining: no jars, cans or bottles on the table. As she likes to say, food always tastes better from a serving platter than from a disposable tin.

Distinguish Yourself

We're famous in our neighborhood for our Israeli salad course at Shabbos lunch. The idea comes from my sister-in-law Chanie, a true-blue Israeli. I figured that imitation is the truest form of praise. If an Israeli course is not your shtick, pick a signature dish or course from your background. Or appropriate someone else's like I did. Transylvania is a long way from Tel Aviv, but come to my house for Shabbos lunch and you would never know it.

Gourmet Salads

My mother is a sheer genius when it comes to salads. Follow her lead and choose unusual and/or tropical fruits like pomegranates, mangos, and donut peaches. Cut them up and dust with some confectioners' sugar for that tropical island feel. Mom goes for glamorous greens, too, and somehow they always taste special. She swears it's her salad bowl – a big, wooden thing that seems to bring the flavor out of a simple blend of mixed field greens, fresh garlic, salt and olive oil. Try it.

No Excuses

Never make disclaimers or excuses for your cooking. Usually you are pointing out things that otherwise would have gone unnoticed. Remember your guests are not at your table as *New York Times* food critics. They're in your home to enjoy the company and conversation.

Clean The Kitchen, If Necessary

If the kitchen is in full view of your dining room, make sure it's spotless. If it's behind closed doors, it's okay with me if it looks like a hurricane hit it. Of course, there's always the chance your guests will try to help clear the table. If you don't want to block the doorway, desperately insisting that they leave it to you, ("No, no, please! I'll take care of it later!") you might want to straighten up a little.

Smile And Say Thanks

Don't protest and don't be excessively humble when people compliment you. A genuine "thank you" goes a long way.

Appetizers:
Drop the Phone and Start Entertaining Like a Pro

If my somewhat privileged upbringing didn't make me a delivery fiend, then moving to Manhattan certainly did. The beauty of delivery is that you never have to get out of your PJs, or your bed, for that matter, to get your daily chow. You can do all your grocery shopping over the phone. In NYC, you can get anything delivered, from a pack of gum to a six-course dinner, plus the toothpick. I would call the deli across the street two or three times a night, ordering one item at a time. Everyone did. It's a way of life.

What an adjustment moving out to the 'burbs has been! After several frustrating attempts at ordering a dial-up dinner, I discovered that 90 percent of the restaurants don't deliver. They offer take-out, which means you have to actually get in your car and go pick it up. Listen, if I'm going to do that, I might as well eat at the restaurant.

The thing about always getting delivery is that you never seriously consider entertaining. And believe me, I was totally fine with that. I was beyond fine; I reveled in the fact that inviting a bunch of people over to my place for dinner was totally not my thing.

Surprise! Now that I have done it, I love it. I really get such pleasure out of entertaining. I'm not talking about entertaining in that stuffy, posh way, where you invite two or three couples and outdo yourself by getting the most expensive caterer. I'm talking about having my apartment overflowing with people – friends, family, friends of friends, family of friends. When people see the food I've prepared and make those "oooh" and "ahhh" noises, I feel a thrill that I used to get when I'd find a pair of shoes that were just the perfect shade of pink.

Beyond the ego boost of numerous compliments, there's a deeper benefit to entertaining. It's the bonding. It's incredibly rewarding to bring family together under one roof – a family

so big and so busy that we'd have trouble keeping up with each other if not for our occasional get-togethers.

When I think of entertaining, I think of appetizers, the ultimate party food. If you get 'em right, you hardly need anything else.

Dips and chips, wraps and rolls, fish from foreign waters and any recipes with the word "cocktail" are good for starters.

The following recipes will get you prepped for any event from a Super Bowl party to an engagement celebration. You'll find elegant apps that women will appreciate and classics that men will wait for at your kitchen door.

PREP: 5 minutes
COOK: none
CHILL: none
YIELD: 6 to 8 servings

Guacamole and Chips

3 ripe Hass avocados, halved and pitted

½ cup chunky salsa

1 teaspoon prepared crushed garlic

2½ tablespoons fresh lemon juice

1½ teaspoons kosher salt

Tortilla chips, for serving

○ Scoop avocados out of skin, place in bowl and mash with fork.

○ Mix in salsa, garlic, lemon juice and salt.

○ Place in the center of a platter and surround with tortilla chips.

If not serving immediately, try this trick for slowing the natural browning process: bury 1 or 2 avocado pits in the guacamole and refrigerate, covered with plastic wrap. My friend Anita told me it psyches out the little avocados – they think they're still in their skins! Whatever the scientific reason, it works.

Stuffed Mushrooms

PREP: 9 minutes

COOK: 15 minutes

CHILL: none

YIELD: 4 servings

1   (10-ounce) carton whole white mushrooms

2   tablespoons plain bread crumbs

2   tablespoons olive oil

$^1/_4$ teaspoon oregano

1   teaspoon prepared crushed garlic

$^1/_4$ teaspoon salt

$^1/_8$ teaspoon black pepper

○ Preheat oven to 425° F.

○ Wipe mushrooms with a damp paper towel to clean. Remove stems and set aside; place mushrooms, rounded side down, in a 9 x 13-inch pan.

○ Chop stems into small pieces and place in bowl.

○ Add bread crumbs, olive oil, oregano, garlic, salt and pepper. Mix well.

○ Place 1 teaspoon of the mixture in each mushroom.

○ Bake, uncovered, at 425° for 15 minutes, until topping is slightly browned.

○ Sprinkle each stuffed mushroom with shredded mozzarella or grated parmesan cheese for a dairy meal.

Cocktail Meatballs

PREP: 12 minutes
COOK: 45 to 50 minutes
CHILL: none
YIELD: 8 servings

1   pound ground beef

1   egg

2   tablespoons bread crumbs

¼   cup seltzer or club soda

1   teaspoon garlic powder

1   teaspoon salt

½   teaspoon black pepper

For Sauce:

1   (15-ounce) can whole cranberry
    sauce

1   (12-ounce) bottle chili sauce

    Rice pilaf, cooked according to
    package directions (optional)

○ Place beef, egg, bread crumbs, seltzer or
   soda, garlic powder, salt and pepper in a
   bowl. Mix lightly but well to combine all
   ingredients.

○ Shape into ¾-inch round balls, using
   your hands, a melon baller or a small
   scoop. Don't over-handle them, though,
   or they'll get tough. Set aside.

○ In a 2- to 3-quart saucepan, heat cranberry
   sauce and chili sauce over medium heat,
   stirring to combine. Bring to a simmer.

○ Drop meatballs into sauce. Return to a
   simmer. Cook, covered, for 45 minutes.

○ Serve with a toothpick in each meatball
   or over rice pilaf if desired.

○ For the ultimate do-ahead tip: Prepare
   meatballs, place on trays and freeze.
   When they're frozen, transfer to sealable
   plastic bags, pop back into the freezer
   and use as needed.

27

PREP: 5 minutes
COOK: 45 minutes to 1 hour
CHILL: none
YIELD: 8 servings

Deli Roll

1   frozen puff pastry sheet (from a
     17.3-ounce package), defrosted
⅓   cup deli mustard
4   ounces (¼ pound) sliced pastrami
4   ounces (¼ pound) sliced turkey
4   ounces (¼ pound) sliced corned
     beef
1   egg, beaten
2   tablespoons sesame seeds

○ Preheat oven to 350° F. Lightly grease a
  12 x 15-inch cookie sheet with non-stick
  cooking spray.

○ Unfold puff pastry sheet onto prepared
  cookie sheet.

○ Spread mustard over pastry sheet.

○ Place meats over sheet in layers, first
  pastrami, then turkey and corned beef.

○ Roll dough as for a jelly roll, place seam
  side down and brush with beaten egg.

○ Sprinkle with sesame seeds.

○ Bake, uncovered, at 350° for 45 minutes
  to 1 hour, until slightly browned and flak-
  ing. Let stand 5 minutes before slicing
  and serving.

I never heard of deli rolls until I hit the
kosher Shabbos scene. It was apparent
that everyone I visited knew how to
make them. So I figured I'd better learn
if I wanted to be really kosher. I found
out later that the dish has no real con-
nection to Judaism, no mystical powers
or deep significance. It just seems to
have become a Shabbos standard in
many homes.

Brush with duck sauce instead of egg
for a hint of sweetness.

Sausage Bites

2   pounds sausage or hot dogs, cut
     into 1-inch pieces

1   cup ketchup

1/3 cup light brown sugar, packed

1/4 cup bourbon

1/2 (10-ounce) bag frozen chopped
     onions or 1 large onion, chopped

1/2 cup water

○ Preheat oven to 350° F.

○ Place meat in a 9 x 13-inch pan with
   ketchup, brown sugar, bourbon, onions
   and water. Mix well to coat.

○ Bake, uncovered, at 350° for 40 minutes.
   Serve with a toothpick in each piece.

Grandma Martha's friend Joan is
responsible for this luscious recipe.
The bourbon aroma and flavor will
immediately get the attention of the
men at your table.

Create a great hors d'oeuvre platter
by serving Sausage Bites with Cocktail
Meatballs (page 27).

PREP: 5 minutes
COOK: 2 hours
CHILL: 4 hours
YIELD: 8 servings

Classic Gefilte Fish

20   baby carrots
2   large onions, chopped coarsely
10   cups water
1   teaspoon salt
1/8 teaspoon coarse black pepper
1   (22-ounce) loaf frozen gefilte fish

○ Place carrots, onions, water, salt and pepper in a 4-quart soup pot, cover and bring
to a boil.

○ When water boils, add fish in parchment
paper and return to boil; immediately
lower heat to simmer.

○ Simmer, uncovered, for 2 hours.

○ Drain in colander, transfer fish to sealable
container and remove parchment paper
by unrolling. Add carrots and onions to
container.

○ Cover and refrigerate until cold, at least
4 hours.

○ Serve sliced with carrots and onions as
a garnish.

○ The debate is not over whether to serve
gefilte fish, but over what condiments
should accompany it. Both white and
red spicy horseradish come in jars desig-
nated as Strong, Double Strong, Triple
Strong and Clear-Your-Sinuses. Then
there's red sweet horseradish and, of
course, mayonnaise. Chrayonaise, another popular choice, is equal parts red
horseradish mixed with mayo. Here's
a hot tip: Wasabi sauce is the latest
gefilte condiment rage.

○ The colder the fish the better, I think.
About half an hour before the meal, I
slice and arrange the fish on a platter,
and keep it chilling in the refrigerator
until just before serving.

Spiced Gefilte Fish

1 (22-ounce) loaf frozen gefilte fish

1 (10-ounce) bag frozen chopped onions

1 (1-pound) bag frozen crinkle cut carrots

2 stalks fresh celery, chopped

¼ teaspoon dried dill weed or 1 sprig fresh dill

¼ teaspoon dried parsley flakes or 2 sprigs fresh parsley

¼ teaspoon celery seed

⅛ teaspoon dried thyme or 1 sprig fresh thyme

⅛ teaspoon ground allspice

8-10 capers

¼ teaspoon salt

¼ teaspoon black pepper

2 cups water

○ Preheat oven to 350°F.

○ Line 9 x 5 x 3-inch loaf pan with onions, carrots and celery.

○ Rinse frozen gefilte loaf under water to remove parchment wrapper and place in loaf pan.

○ Sprinkle dill weed, parsley, celery seed, thyme, allspice, capers, salt and pepper evenly over fish. Pour water in loaf pan around sides of fish and cover with foil.

○ Bake at 350° for 2 hours and 30 minutes.

○ Transfer fish and vegetables to a sealable container, cover and refrigerate until cold, at least 4 hours.

Gefilte fish, "the" Jewish food for Shabbos and holiday festivities, was invented by some ingenious Jewish women many generations ago to help diners avoid tangling with bones while they ate. The word itself means "filled" in Yiddish, referring to the original practice of filling the fish's skin with ground fish.

This original recipe comes straight from my recipe tester Joy's father-in-law, a Philly native like me. It offers an interesting, unexpected flavor.

PREP: 4 minutes
COOK: 25 minutes
CHILL: none
YIELD: 8 servings

Sweet and Sour Salmon

8   salmon fillets, about 2 pounds
1   cup Cantonese-style duck sauce
    (Sweet & Sour)
½   cup ketchup
½   teaspoon crushed red pepper flakes

○ Preheat oven to 350° F. Lightly grease a
  9 x 13-inch pan with non-stick cooking
  spray.

○ Rinse fillets and pat dry. Place in prepared pan.

○ In a small bowl, mix the duck sauce,
  ketchup and crushed red pepper and
  pour over salmon.

○ Bake, uncovered, at 350° for 25 minutes
  or until desired doneness. Serve warm.

When we go out to eat, I'll question
the waiter for five minutes about the
different fishes and preparations on
the menu, only to say, "I'll take the
salmon." Of course, I never noticed
I did that until my husband started
teasing me about it. Funny how
you don't realize that you do things
repeatedly until you're married and
there is someone there to point it out
to you, again and again. And again.

Slice zucchini, onions and red and
green bell peppers and place under
salmon before baking.

Cold Smoked Fish Salad

PREP: 6 minutes
COOK: none
CHILL: 1 hour
YIELD: 8 to 10 servings

2   pounds assorted smoked and salted fishes (sable, whitefish, nova and kippered salmon)

1   tablespoon freshly ground or prepared white horseradish

1   teaspoon coarse black pepper

2   tablespoons lemon juice

1   tablespoon minced fresh dill

Seasoned flatbreads or party rye (optional)

○   Cut fish into bite-sized pieces and place in bowl.

○   Add horseradish, pepper and lemon juice, and toss to mix. Garnish with dill and chill for 1 hour before serving. Serve with seasoned flatbreads or party rye, if desired.

This recipe was inspired by English chef Jamie Oliver. His version called for non-kosher shellfish, so this adaptation is for the kosher connoisseur. Smoked fish is a typical Sunday brunch item in many Jewish circles. This is a welcome change from the traditional fish platter.

Chilled Salmon with Dijon Dipping Sauce

8   salmon fillets, about 2 pounds

1   tablespoon dried dill flakes or
      2 tablespoons minced fresh dill

1   tablespoon dried parsley flakes or
      2 tablespoons minced fresh parsley

¼   teaspoon coarse kosher salt

½   teaspoon black pepper

For Sauce:

¾   cup light mayonnaise

2   tablespoons Dijon-style mustard

1   tablespoon lemon juice

1   teaspoon prepared minced garlic

1   tablespoon chopped fresh dill

¼   teaspoon sugar

¼   teaspoon pepper

○ Preheat oven to 450°F. Lightly grease a 9 x 13-inch pan with non-stick cooking spray.

○ Rinse fillets and pat dry. Place in prepared pan.

○ In a small bowl, mix the dill, parsley, salt and pepper.

○ Sprinkle seasoning mixture over each fillet.

○ Bake, uncovered, at 450° for 12 to 15 minutes or until desired doneness.

○ While salmon is cooking, prepare sauce. Place all ingredients in a bowl and mix well to blend.

○ Chill salmon and sauce separately in refrigerator for at least 2 hours before serving. Serve sauce on the side.

This dish comes from my good friend Anita. It's part her invention, part adaptation from *Spice and Spirit*, the fabulous Lubavitch Women's Cookbook by Esther Blau, Tzirrel Deitsch and Cherna Light.

Whip up a Wasabi Scallion Sauce by combining one large bunch of scallions (use only the green part), 1 cup light mayonnaise, the juice of 1 lemon and ⅛ teaspoon wasabi powder. Blend or process until creamy and smooth. Refrigerate overnight to soften the bite.

PREP: 10 minutes

COOK: 30 minutes

CHILL: 1 hour

YIELD: 8 servings

Turkish Salad

1   onion, chopped

1   teaspoon prepared crushed garlic

1   tablespoon olive oil

2   green bell peppers, seeded, veins removed, diced, or 1 (10-ounce) bag stir-fry peppers, defrosted

2   jalapeño hot pepper rings (from a jar)

2   cups canned crushed tomatoes

1   teaspoon salt

¼   teaspoon black pepper

    Quartered pita breads (optional)

- In 10-inch skillet, sauté onion and garlic in oil over medium heat for 2 minutes.

- Add peppers, tomatoes, salt and pepper.

- Bring to a boil. Reduce heat and simmer for 30 minutes. Chill in refrigerator for at least 1 hour. Serve with warm pita bread, if desired.

For a nutritious alternative to dipping with bread, I serve baby carrots and celery sticks with hummus, tahini and Turkish salad.

Add sautéed zucchini and eggplant and you have a ratatouille. Serve it warm as a deliciously thick and flavorful side dish.

Tahini

½ cup sesame paste (tahini)

¼ cup water

1 tablespoon lemon juice

2 cloves garlic, peeled

1 teaspoon parsley flakes

1 teaspoon salt

○ Place tahini, water, lemon juice, garlic, parsley and salt in food processor.

○ Blend well, until thin and creamy; chill in refrigerator for 1 hour before serving.

We use tahini on everything. It's our go-to Israeli condiment. I like it on salads and my husband even smothers his pizza in the stuff. Initially, I was appalled when he did that. Now he has to bring home extra tahini from the pizza shop. It's for me!

Serve a few spoonfuls atop the middle of a hummus platter.

Hummus

1 (15-ounce) can chickpeas, drained
⅓ cup sesame paste (tahini)
2 cloves garlic, peeled
   Juice of ½ lemon (about 2 tablespoons)
2½ teaspoons salt
1 cup water
   Quartered pita breads (optional)

○ Pour chickpeas into food processor.

○ Add sesame paste, garlic, lemon juice and salt.

○ Blend in food processor, adding water slowly until desired thickness – a dip-like consistency – is reached.

○ Chill in refrigerator for 1 hour before serving. Arrange on a plate with warm pita bread, if desired.

Like me, you probably buy the elements to an Israeli salad course – hummus, tahini, Turkish salad and all the rest – already prepared. There's nothing wrong with that, but if you have the time, you can make some of them fresh with these authentic Middle Eastern recipes, courtesy of my sister-in-law Chanie. They've been passed down straight from her Iraqi grandmother to her mother, to her, to me, and now to you.

Serve on a flat plate and use the back of a spoon in a circular motion to smooth out the hummus. Top with a few dashes of sumac or paprika, and drizzle with olive oil.

Charif

PREP: 4 minutes; slightly longer
if using fresh tomatoes

COOK: none

CHILL: 1 hour

YIELD: 8 servings

1   (20-ounce) can whole tomatoes,
    drained, or 5 tomatoes, quartered

¼   cup white vinegar

½   cup oil

1   tablespoon prepared or fresh
    chopped garlic

1   tablespoon lemon juice

1   teaspoon cumin

1½ teaspoons kosher salt

1   teaspoon cayenne pepper or to taste

4   jalapeño hot pepper rings (from a jar)
    Quartered pita breads (optional)

○ Combine tomatoes, vinegar, oil, garlic,
  lemon juice, cumin, salt, cayenne and
  peppers in a blender or food processor
  and pulse until smooth.

○ Chill in refrigerator for 1 hour.

○ Serve as a dip with warm pita bread,
  if desired.

Charif is the Hebrew word for sharp –
and boy, does this recipe have a kick!
It's not for the faint of heart. But that's
the beauty of preparing a dish like this
from scratch. You can make it mild or
burning hot.

PREP: 5 minutes

COOK: 1 to 2 minutes

CHILL: none

YIELD: 3 to 4 servings

Crispy Artichoke Hearts

1   cup seasoned bread crumbs

1   (12-ounce) jar quartered, marinated
     artichoke hearts

1½ cups extra virgin olive oil

1½ cups vegetable oil

○ Place bread crumbs in a small bowl.

○ Drain artichokes and toss in bread crumbs
   to cover. Set aside.

○ Heat olive and vegetable oils in a deep
   10-inch skillet over medium heat. Temperature should reach 350° to 375°F on
   a deep-fry thermometer, or a bread cube
   tossed in should brown in 60 seconds.

○ Add artichokes carefully. Fry 1 to 2 minutes
   until crisp.

○ With a slotted spoon, remove artichokes
   from hot oil. Drain on paper towels and
   serve immediately. Place a decorative
   toothpick in each piece, if desired.

○ Handle artichokes very delicately to
   ensure that the bread crumbs don't
   fall off.

Soup du Jour

My family loves soup. Thick and creamy, hearty or light, cold or piping hot — we're just into soups. I was raised on it as a main dish, as a side course, as dessert. So I figured it would be a snap to prepare. After all, it's mostly water, isn't it?

Chicken soup is a traditional component of the Friday night Shabbos meal. The first Shabbos after I was married,

I invited my mother, sister and grandfather over for dinner. Knowing my total lack of culinary prowess, they came early to lend moral support and guidance in the kitchen. You should have seen it: There was my 85-year-old grandfather, in his chef's apron, complaining about my knives and pots. ("You expect me to work with this? What's this made of, *plastic?*") My mother and I bossed each other around as if we knew what we were doing. ("You need more water in that pot." "Aren't there supposed to be greens?") Everyone's voice was raised. (In our family, we don't yell; we just talk loud.) Smoke was rising from the oven and pots were boiling over.

That night, I served the soup to my new husband. It was an oily concoction with tons of vegetables – none of which I had cut. Not knowing his food preferences too well at that point, I asked Hubby if he liked veggies in his soup and he assured me that he liked everything. So I really gave him *everything*. I gave him a whole carrot and a parsnip the size of my forearm. He also got two stalks of celery, a whole onion and so much parsley you could hardly see the soup. I remember holding my breath as I served it to him, so proud that I had cooked a soup, my first soup with my own hands just for him. I can't even remember the expression on his face. I think I've blocked it out for life.

But there was a silver lining to this fiasco. My husband, who had some experience working for caterers, decided it was time to take charge. That week we went shopping and bought

knives that even my grandfather would treasure. Then he showed me how to dice and slice, and cut through a vegetable like a professional chef with a very quick motion and very careful hand placement. He picked up these tricks from his father and from years of hanging out in catering kitchens. Most brides would be embarrassed by cooking lessons from their hubby. Not me. I took his gastronomic expertise as a gift from G-d.

It should come as no surprise that I cook soup year-round, and my whole family clamors for it. My father and grandfather share a totally unscientific theory: Eat hot soup in the summer because it cools you off! First you eat, then you sweat and then you're cool. My husband eats my chicken soup in the summer too, but not because of any such theory. It's simply because he loves it!

This next chapter is filled with exotic and ethnic soups from all around the world, from traditional recipes to original creations. You'll find hearty soups, spicy soups, thick soups, light soups, warm soups made with wine and cold soups made with fruit. With all of these options, you should find a soup to fit every taste bud and every finicky eater. Some of these soups are so good across the board that you will need a big – really big – vat that you can dip into whenever someone asks for "More, please."

PREP: 5 minutes
COOK: 40 to 50 minutes
CHILL: none
YIELD: 8 servings

Butternut Squash Soup

1   medium onion, minced

2   pounds prepared peeled, cubed
       butternut squash

6   cups water

1   cup canned coconut milk

½   cup white wine

2   cloves garlic, chopped or 2 frozen
       crushed garlic cubes

1   tablespoon fresh grated ginger or
       1 teaspoon ginger powder

1   teaspoon curry powder

¼   teaspoon dried thyme

1   teaspoon kosher salt

○ Place all ingredients in a 6-quart stockpot.
   Cover and bring to a boil.

○ Reduce to simmer and cook, covered,
   for 30 to 40 minutes, until squash is soft.

○ Use a potato masher or a fork to mash
   squash and continue cooking for 10 minutes.

○ Ladle into bowls and serve.

49

Squash, gourds and all things orange
seem especially appealing in the fall,
when they are like the colors of the
falling leaves. This recipe was inspired
by one in *Food and Wine* magazine.
Their version was so time-consuming
and complicated, I nearly skipped
it entirely. (The first instruction practically had you growing the butternut
squash and plucking it from the field.)
I prefer this quicker way to get to
the same goal. The result is a light
and creamy soup, with just a hint of
sweetness.

One thing I skipped, but go for it if
you have the time and patience: Purée
the soup in batches in the blender.

To peel ginger, use a sharp paring
knife. Remove the rough, bumpy skin
about as far down as you think you
need to yield the amount called for.
Then grate or mince.

Lentil Soup

10   cups water

1   cup lentils

1   cup red lentils

4   tablespoons Osem Vegetable
     Soup Mix

1   teaspoon garlic powder

1   teaspoon onion powder

1   teaspoon dried parsley or
     1 tablespoon fresh minced
     parsley

½   teaspoon black pepper

1   (10-ounce) bag frozen peas
     and carrots

     Additional fresh parsley, minced
     (optional)

○ Place water, lentils, soup mix, garlic and
onion powders, parsley and black pepper
in a 6-quart stockpot and bring to a boil.

○ Reduce to a simmer, cover and cook for
2 hours and 30 minutes, stirring occasionally.

○ Add peas and carrots, cover and cook for
another 30 minutes. Ladle into bowls and
serve. Garnish with minced fresh parsley
if desired.

○ If refrigerating overnight and reheating,
add 1 to 2 cups of water and mix well to
prevent burning.

○ Serve with hot, crusty French bread
and a salad for an informal lunch.

Purée of Bean and
Vegetable Soup

1	(15-ounce) can white beans, drained
1	(15-ounce) can red kidney beans, drained
1	(15-ounce) can peas and carrots, drained
1	(15-ounce) can sweet corn Niblets, drained
1	(15-ounce) can diced tomatoes, drained
2	cups water
1	cup liquid non-dairy creamer
4	tablespoons olive oil
3	tablespoons Osem Vegetable Soup Mix
4	frozen crushed garlic cubes or 4 medium garlic cloves

Place all ingredients in blender and purée until smooth. You may have to do this in batches; do not overload blender.

Transfer mixture to a 6-quart stockpot, cover and bring to a simmer over medium heat for 10 minutes or until heated through.

Ladle into bowls and serve warm as a soup, or refrigerate overnight and serve cold as a bean dip.

This soup was inspired by a Hungarian bean dip called *tort paszuli*, which literally means "broken beans." My grandparents used to make it using a painstaking, day-long process. When I asked Uputzi, my 85-year-old grandfather, how to do it, he said it's almost as tiring to give out the recipe as to make it.

Too much work for me! So I had to figure out my own way to make something that was reminiscent of *tort paszuli*. I added a lot of stuff – corn, tomatoes, non-dairy creamer – but the concept was inspired by their years of hard work and my memories of a taste I craved.

Anyhow, I served the "*tort paszuli*" I made to my mother and sister, never dreaming they would suspect its origins. I didn't say a word, and they both said it reminded them of Ma and Uputzi's *tort paszuli*! Victory!

Whether serving hot or cold, slice and sauté a few onions in olive oil until golden brown and place a spoonful in each bowl or in the center of a platter.

Asian Shiitake Mushroom Soup

PREP: 10 minutes

COOK: 50 minutes

CHILL: none

YIELD: 4 to 6 servings

2   (3.5-ounce) cartons sliced shiitake
     mushrooms

8   cups water

1   tablespoon Osem Consommé Mix

1   tablespoon Osem Mushroom
     Soup Mix

¾   cup dry white wine

1   leek, washed and sliced; use just
     white part, about ½ cup

2   teaspoons grated fresh ginger or
     1 teaspoon ground ginger

1½   teaspoons toasted sesame oil

¼   cup fresh minced parsley or
     1 tablespoon dried parsley

1   tablespoon minced fresh dill or
     1 teaspoon dried dill

4   frozen crushed garlic cubes

½   teaspoon sea salt

○ Place all ingredients in a 6-quart
   stockpot.

○ Cover and bring to a boil. Reduce to
   a simmer and cook for 50 minutes.

○ Ladle into bowls and serve.

For a heartier soup, skin and shred 2
poached chicken breasts and add for
last 10 minutes of cooking. Or add a
handful of rice sticks for last 4 to 5
minutes of cooking.

Beef Porridge

1   tablespoon olive oil

1   (2-pound) flanken

1   large onion, chopped

12   cups water

1   (6-ounce) sleeve split pea soup
     mix with spice packet

1   (6-ounce) sleeve barley and lima
     bean soup mix with spice packet

15   baby carrots

1   teaspoon sea salt

2   stalks celery, cut in ¼ inch slices

In a 6-quart stockpot, heat olive oil over medium heat.

Rinse meat and pat dry. Season with salt and pepper.

Place flanken and onions in pot and cook over medium heat for 2 to 3 minutes until meat is lightly browned on both sides.

Add remaining ingredients, cover and bring to boil. Skim off any foam that rises to the surface and discard.

Reduce heat to a simmer and cook, uncovered for 3 hours, stirring occasionally. Ladle into bowls and serve.

If refrigerating overnight and reheating, add 1 to 2 cups of water and mix well to prevent burning.

A Geller Classic, passed down from Grandma Martha, this is a perfect winter soup. It was by special request that I learned how to make it and it took me only five tries to master. It's worth the trouble. Hubby used to ask his grandma, "Could you make both chicken and porridge for Shabbos, so I can have a ladle of each in my bowl?" Now he tries the same shtick with me. I haven't been daring enough to try the combination of the two – yet.

After cooking for 3 hours, the flanken gets so soft it just melts in your mouth. This hearty soup could be a meal with a nice, thick slice of challah.

PREP: 11 minutes

COOK: 18 to 20 minutes

CHILL: none

YIELD: 8 servings

Italian Bean Soup

1   medium onion, quartered

8   cups water

¾   cup dry red wine

1   (14.5-ounce) can chopped tomatoes

1   (15-ounce) can white beans,
    not drained

1   (15-ounce) can red kidney beans,
    not drained

1   (15-ounce) can chickpeas, drained

10 baby carrots

10 baby zucchini

2   teaspoons Osem Vegetable Soup Mix

1   frozen crushed garlic cube

1   teaspoon dried oregano

1   tablespoon kosher salt

½   teaspoon coarse black pepper

○ Place all ingredients in a 6-quart stockpot. Cover and bring to a boil.

○ Reduce to a simmer and cook, uncovered,
   for 18 to 20 minutes.

○ Ladle into bowls and serve.

○ The wine and oregano give this tomato-
   based bean soup a distinctive flavor.
   You'll find it's a bit spicy and slightly
   smoky.

Turkey Mushroom Soup

PREP: 5 minutes
COOK: 2 hours, 30 minutes
CHILL: none
YIELD: 8 to 10 servings

2   turkey wings, about ¾ pound each, rinsed and cleaned

10 cups water

1   (4-ounce) carton dried mushrooms

1   tablespoon olive oil

10-12 small white mushrooms

10 baby carrots

½   cup dried split peas

½   cup lima beans

1   cup barley

1   tablespoon Osem Consommé Mix

1   (6-ounce) sleeve bean soup mix and seasoning packet

    Pumpernickel bread sliced thickly (optional)

- Place turkey wings, water, dried mushrooms, oil, white mushrooms, carrots, peas, beans, barley and soup mix in a 6-quart stockpot and bring to boil.

- Reduce to a simmer, cover and cook for 2 hours and 30 minutes.

- Ladle into bowls and serve with thick slices of pumpernickel bread if desired.

- If refrigerating overnight and reheating, add 1 to 2 cups of water and mix well to prevent burning.

My stepmother-in-law Judy gave me many wedding gifts, but the one I thought I'd never, ever use was the cookbook from the Hebrew Academy of the Five Towns and Rockaway *(HAFTR)*. Now I am wild about several recipes from it, and a variation on this soup is one of them. It's hearty and "eats like a meal." I'm also happy that it is made with turkey instead of red meat.

If you have extra time, sauté 10 to 12 fresh mushrooms of your choice and use them as a garnish on each bowl.

1	pound stew beef, cubed
1	tablespoon olive oil
1	(16-ounce) bag shredded white cabbage
1	(16-ounce) can crushed tomatoes
2	cups tomato sauce
3	cups water
2	tablespoons lemon juice
2	tablespoons white vinegar
$\frac{1}{2}$	cup light brown sugar, packed
$\frac{1}{4}$	cup granulated sugar
$\frac{1}{2}$	teaspoon onion powder
1	tablespoon sea salt

Rinse meat and pat dry. In a 6-quart stockpot, heat olive oil and brown beef over medium heat for 2 minutes, stirring.

Add cabbage, tomatoes and tomato sauce, water, lemon juice, vinegar, both sugars, onion powder and salt.

Bring to a boil. Skim off any foam and discard.

Reduce to a simmer, cover and cook for at least 2 hours. Longer is fine; you really want the flavors to mellow. Ladle into bowls and serve.

This recipe is a classic. When I put the word out that I was doing a cookbook, I got three versions of it and I rolled them all into one. We tested it on a bunch of 14-year-old boys and they were licking their bowls and asking for seconds.

Avgolemono Soup

PREP: 7 minutes
COOK: 30 to 35 minutes
CHILL: none
YIELD: 6 to 8 servings

61

3   (15-ounce) cans chicken broth
8½   cups water
1½   teaspoons salt
1   cup white rice
3   eggs
       Juice of 3 lemons (6 tablespoons
       fresh lemon juice)

○ Place chicken broth, water and salt in a
  4- to 6-quart soup pot. Bring to a boil.

○ Add rice, cover and simmer for 20 minutes.

○ When rice is cooked, remove pot from heat.

○ Place eggs in a bowl and beat well. Beat
  in lemon juice.

○ While continuing to beat eggs vigorously,
  ladle out about 1 cup of chicken broth
  and beat it into the eggs. Pour egg and
  broth mixture back into the pot.

○ Return pot to heat and stir while broth
  thickens, but do not let boil. Ladle into
  bowls and serve.

○ This easy soup, a Greek favorite, can
  be made out of ingredients you usually
  have in the house.

Griz Galuska (Hungarian Farina Soup Dumplings)

PREP: 4 minutes
COOK: 40 minutes
CHILL: 30 minutes
YIELD: 5 servings

1   egg
2   tablespoons plus 2 teaspoons farina
¼   teaspoon salt
1   teaspoon olive oil
1   chicken consommé stock cube
5   cups water

In a bowl, mix egg, farina, salt and olive oil until well combined. Let stand 30 minutes, either in refrigerator or at room temperature, until firm.

Place water and soup cube in a 4-quart stockpot and bring to a boil.

Using a tablespoon, scoop up farina mixture and drop in soup. Repeat, placing as many dumplings as you can in the pot without crowding.

Lower heat to a slow, rolling boil (too strong a boil will cause dumplings to fall apart).

Cook 15 to 20 minutes, or until a dumpling cut in half is no longer yellow on the inside. Repeat until finished with all the batter.

Place 2 to 3 dumplings in each bowl of your favorite soup and serve.

Farina dumplings are the Hungarian version of matzoh balls. A wonderful addition to a chicken, beef or tomato soup, they are so tasty that you may find yourself working them into your regular repertoire.

If not serving immediately, place dumplings and some of the broth (just enough to keep them moist) in a sealable container and store in the fridge.

Classic Chicken Soup

1   (3½-pound) chicken, cut into 8 pieces

12   cups water

1   large carrot, peeled, cut into bite-sized pieces

1   large parsnip, peeled, cut into bite-sized pieces

1   large onion, cut into bite-sized pieces

1   large turnip, peeled, cut into bite-sized pieces

4   medium stalks of celery, cut into bite-sized pieces

1   bouquet garni of 15 parsley sprigs, 15 dill sprigs, 1 tablespoon whole peppercorns

3   tablespoons Osem Consommé Mix

1   (½-ounce) chicken consommé stock cube

    Additional fresh parsley or dill, for garnish (optional)

PREP: 15 minutes
COOK: 1 hour 45 minutes
CHILL: none
YIELD: 6 to 8 servings

Rinse chicken and place in a 6-quart soup pot.

Add water and bring to a boil over high heat. Skim any foam, residue or fat that rises to the surface using a large spoon or skimmer and discard.

Once boiling, reduce heat to a simmer and add carrot, parsnip, onion, turnip, celery, bouquet garni, consommé mix and stock cube.

Simmer, covered, for 1 hour and 30 minutes.

Remove the bouquet garni.

Remove chicken from bone and place a few pieces into each bowl. Ladle soup and vegetables over chicken.

Mince dill or parsley and sprinkle on immediately before serving, if desired. Or cool the soup and refrigerate overnight. Skim off any fat that rises to the top before reheating.

Everyone agrees it's not a Jewish holiday meal, or a Jewish cookbook, without chicken soup!

Chicken soup is the classic Jewish food. It's the healer of all things from a cold to a broken heart. There are 101 different ways to make it, and in my opinion, they're all good, although everyone thinks their bubby's is the best! Just be sure you make enough so everyone can have seconds or even thirds.

Avoid having to fish peppercorns out of your dishes by using a bouquet garni — a little bundle of herbs — to flavor stews and broths. Just place the herbs in a small muslin bag or piece of cheesecloth and tie securely with cotton string.

PREP: 9 minutes
COOK: none
CHILL: 2 hours
YIELD: 4 servings

Mango Strawberry Soup

4   mangos, peeled and pitted

1   cup fresh strawberries,
    washed and stems removed

2   cups liquid non-dairy creamer

½   cup white wine

1   teaspoon pure vanilla extract

    Mint leaves, for garnish (optional)

○ In a blender, place mangos, strawberries,
   creamer, wine and vanilla; blend until
   smooth and creamy, about 1 to 2 minutes.

○ Chill for 2 hours before serving.

○ Ladle into bowls and garnish with mint
   leaves if desired.

This is not only a fruit soup, it's amazing as a sauce over ice cream! Serve it cold as an app, or drizzle a few spoonfuls of it over pound cake and a scoop of ice cream for dessert. It's one of those wonderful, versatile things that will work for you in lots of ways.

Salads:
It's Easy Being Green

Even before I finish breakfast, I'm thinking about my lunchtime salad. You might not believe me when I say I'm a salad fiend because I've already told you that soup is my favorite course. So the true confession – which you will realize anyway before the end of this book — is that I love food, all food. I'm not so much a good cook as I am a good eater! That's the source of my recipe instincts and my salad creativity. I like playing with combinations you would expect and combinations you wouldn't dare to consider. If it's in the supermarket, it's in one of my salads.

Maybe the main reason I'm into salads is the dressing. If you love it as much as I do, there will be more dressing than greens on your plate. So you will find lots of recipes for dressings in this chapter. I always prepare my salads and dressings ahead of the meal. But unless the recipe calls for marinating, I toss or mix them right before serving. That way, the salads are ready to go in a flash, but they don't get mushy or lose their freshness.

Serving salads to lots of guests, I've discovered a surprising thing: Contrary to popular notion, salads do cross the gender line. True, some salads seem to go over better with one group than the other. Women gravitate to my Crunchy Tofu Thai Salad, while men tend to scoop up more Israeli Salad. But some salads are definitely equal opportunity. A garden salad layered in a trifle bowl is such an exquisite crowd-pleaser that even men, real men —you know, the ones who build things — have commented on its taste and colorful beauty.

Establishing your own signature style is fun. You become known for that one special dish or perhaps a few unique recipes, due

to their originality or because they're made "just right." As a new, clueless-on-cuisine bride, I was delighted to learn that I could distinguish myself in the kitchen without even turning on the stove. Better yet, 90 percent of my specialty was store-bought. The salad course was the answer to my prayers.

For tips on selecting the best fruits and vegetables, read my interview with the produce department manager at Super-sol supermarket on page 252.

Avocado and Seared Tuna Steak Salad

PREP: 12 minutes
COOK: 4 minutes
CHILL: none
YIELD: 4 to 6 servings

1   tablespoon olive oil

2   pounds tuna steak

1½   teaspoons kosher salt

½   teaspoon black pepper

2   red onions, peeled and diced

2   scallions, white and half
       of the green part (about
       6 inches), sliced

2   ripe Hass avocados, peeled,
       pitted and diced

For Dressing:

4   tablespoons olive oil

1½   teaspoons wasabi powder

4   tablespoons lime juice

10   dashes Tabasco sauce
       (about ½ teaspoon)

1   teaspoon dried coriander
       or 1 tablespoon fresh minced
       cilantro

○ Heat olive oil in a 12-inch skillet over
   medium-high heat.

○ Rinse tuna, pat dry and rub with salt and
   pepper.

○ Sauté 2 minutes on each side, until seared.
   Tuna should be cooked on outside and
   still raw inside. Set aside.

○ In a small sauce pan, combine dressing
   ingredients and warm over medium-
   low heat.

○ Place onions, scallions and avocado in
   salad bowl.

○ Cut tuna into 1-inch chunks and add
   to bowl.

○ Pour dressing over salad. Serve at
   room temperature.

We can thank Aunt Tamara for this
recipe. She probably thought her version
was quick, but it wasn't quick enough
for a novice like me. I've revised it
slightly to make the prep time even
shorter.

A dash means a quick shake of the
Tabasco bottle.

69

Sweet Tuna Salad

PREP: 5 minutes
COOK: none
CHILL: 1 hour
YIELD: 4 servings

2   (6-ounce) cans tuna fish packed in water, drained
¼   cup sweet relish
¼   cup canned sweet yellow corn Niblets
⅓   cup mayonnaise
⅓   cup honey Dijon-style mustard
    Assorted crackers (optional)

○ Place tuna, relish, corn, mayonnaise and mustard in a medium salad bowl.

○ Mash and mix with a fork until blended well.

○ Chill in refrigerator for 1 hour before serving.

○ Arrange on platter and surround with crackers, if desired.

My best friend Rozanna made this one up when she was studying in England. When I went to visit her, she presented me with what seemed like a weird dish. "Just try it" she urged, and I've been a sweet tuna fan ever since. Her flatmate had the cutest English accent, pronouncing tuna as "chuna." I hear her saying "chuna" every time I make this.

Sun-Dried Tomato Caesar Salad

PREP: 9 minutes
COOK: none
CHILL: none
YIELD: 6 servings

2 romaine hearts, shredded about ¼-inch thick

½ cup croutons

½ cup sun-dried tomatoes in oil, chopped

Grape tomatoes, halved (optional)

For Dressing:

¼ cup light mayonnaise

¼ cup olive oil

¾ tablespoon Dijon-style mustard

1 tablespoon Worcestershire sauce *(see note, p. 139)*

3 cubes frozen crushed garlic, or 3 cloves fresh garlic, minced

1 tablespoon dried parsley or 2 tablespoons fresh minced parsley

1 tablespoon onion powder

2 tablespoons water

¼ teaspoon kosher salt

½ teaspoon coarse black pepper

○ Place romaine in a large salad bowl.

○ Add croutons and sun-dried tomatoes.

○ In a separate bowl, whisk together dressing ingredients until smooth and creamy.

○ Pour over salad and toss lightly.

○ Serve immediately with grape tomatoes, if desired.

Although sun-dried tomatoes are not traditional ingredients for Caesar salad, they're perfect at my table because I love tomatoes and my husband doesn't. He can pick around them and we're both happy. The idea comes from our favorite restaurant, Bistro Grill in Woodmere, New York.

Using this recipe at a dairy meal allows for the addition of fresh grated parmesan, a traditional ingredient in Caesar salad. And don't underestimate the power of homemade Herb Seasoned Croutons (page 92), the ideal complement to Caesar salad.

Baby Spinach and Portobello Mushroom Salad

1   tablespoon olive oil

1   (6-ounce) package sliced
     portobello mushrooms

1   (10-ounce) package baby
     spinach leaves

1   red onion, thinly sliced

10   grape tomatoes, halved

For Dressing:

⅓   cup olive oil

2   tablespoons balsamic vinegar

2   tablespoons mayonnaise

1   teaspoon prepared minced garlic

½   teaspoon sugar

½   teaspoon kosher salt

○ In a 12-inch skillet, heat oil over medium heat.

○ Add mushrooms and sauté for 5 minutes. Set aside.

○ Place baby spinach, onion and tomatoes in a salad bowl.

○ In a small bowl, whisk together all the dressing ingredients until smooth and creamy. Pour over salad.

○ Spoon mushrooms over salad. Toss gently and serve.

75

If you don't have time to sauté, just use 1 carton of fresh sliced white mushrooms in place of the portobellos.

Warm Salmon Salad

2	tablespoons olive oil
1½	pounds salmon fillet, skinned and cut into bite-sized pieces
½	red bell pepper, seeded, veins removed, diced
½	green, yellow or orange bell pepper, seeded, veins removed, diced
½	cup golden raisins
¼	cup pine nuts
½	teaspoon salt
1	(10-ounce) package baby spinach
½	cup bottled balsamic vinaigrette dressing

○ In a 12-inch skillet, heat olive oil over medium heat. Add salmon, peppers, raisins, pine nuts and salt.

○ Sauté for 7 to 8 minutes, until salmon is opaque and peppers are tender.

○ Place baby spinach in a salad bowl and spoon warm salmon mixture over spinach.

○ Drizzle balsamic dressing over the salad and serve warm or at room temperature.

○ Use the dressing from the Warm Pepper and Craisin Salad (page 89) instead of bottled dressing if you have time to make it.

Sweet Carrot Salad

PREP: 7 minutes
COOK: none
CHILL: none
YIELD: 4 servings

1   (10-ounce) package shredded carrots

¼   cup packaged shredded red cabbage

½   cup raisins

¼   cup orange-flavored Craisins or dried cranberries

¼   cup crushed pineapple, drained, or ½ cup fresh pineapple, diced

½   cup dried apricots, quartered

2   tablespoons orange juice

2   tablespoons honey

¼   cup canola oil

¼   teaspoon cinnamon

⅛   teaspoon nutmeg

○ Place carrots, cabbage, raisins, Craisins, pineapple, apricots, juice, honey, oil, cinnamon and nutmeg in a salad bowl.

○ Toss well to mix. Serve chilled or at room temperature.

The pineapples, cranberries and apricots in this salad look like shining jewels. And of course, the taste matches their beauty.

Mexican Taco Salad

PREP: 7 minutes

COOK: none

CHILL: none

YIELD: 12 servings

2 romaine hearts, shredded about ¼-inch thick

2 stalks celery, diced

½ cup packaged shredded carrots

1 (15-ounce) can black beans, rinsed and drained

1 (15-ounce) can sweet yellow corn Niblets, drained

1 cup light mayonnaise

½ cup prepared chunky salsa

1 cup crushed tortilla chips

1 ripe Hass avocado, peeled, pitted and diced

○ Place romaine, celery, carrots, black beans and corn in a large salad bowl.

○ Mix mayonnaise and salsa in a small bowl and add to salad.

○ Add chips and avocado, and toss lightly. Serve immediately so the chips don't get too soggy or the avocados mushy.

You could call this one a community effort. I tried a version of this dish at my friend Tzipora's house. She uses chopped sautéed meat in place of the tortilla chips (kind of like the low-carb version). I got the dressing from my sister-in-law Debbie, and added a few touches of my own.

Try crushed hard tacos in place of or in addition to tortilla chips. For a heartier version, add chopped meat sautéed with Mexican spices.

California Avocado Salad

1   (11-ounce) can sweet yellow corn
    Niblets, drained

1   (11-ounce) can white shoepeg corn,
    drained

2   ripe Hass avocados, peeled, pitted
    and diced

1/2 (15-ounce) can hearts of palm,
    drained and cut into bite-sized
    pieces

15 grape tomatoes, halved

1/2 small red onion, thinly sliced

2   tablespoons olive oil

2   tablespoons toasted sesame oil

2   tablespoons ume plum vinegar

2   tablespoons seasoned rice vinegar

○ Place corn, avocados, hearts of palm,
  tomatoes, onion, oils and vinegars in a
  medium salad bowl.

○ Toss lightly (you don't want avocados
  to get mushy) and serve at room temperature.

Ume plum vinegar is an Asian vinegar and can be found in the specialty
food aisle of your local supermarket or
health food store. (It usually will not
be lumped together with the other
vinegars.) It has a pungent and salty
taste, though, so use it sparingly. If
you are watching your sodium intake,
substitute additional seasoned rice
vinegar. Then season lightly with
salt to taste.

I got the inspiration for this recipe from
Donna, a friend of a friend. I call it California Avocado Salad because she's
from California.

Long Grain and Wild Rice Salad

1   (6-ounce) box Near East Long
      Grain and Wild Rice, cooked
      according to package directions

⅓   cup Craisins or dried cranberries

2   tablespoons fresh minced parsley

½   medium red onion, minced

1   large celery stalk, diced

3   tablespoons olive oil

2   tablespoons white vinegar

○ While rice is cooking, mix Craisins, parsley, onion, celery, olive oil and vinegar
   in a large bowl.

○ Add rice to bowl while still hot and
   mix well.

○ Cover and chill in refrigerator at least
   4 hours or up to 1 day.

It bothered my recipe tester, Joy, that
we didn't have a rice salad. She said
this book simply wouldn't be complete
without one. "They are so pretty and
easy, and a real crowd pleaser." So in
my search for pretty, easy, rice salads,
I found tons that were pretty, but not
many that were easy. So we adapted a
few to create this delicious version.

One variation would be to use chopped
scallions instead of red onion. Or you
could add 3 tablespoons of slivered almonds for a satisfying crunch. This rice
salad also tastes great made with Near
East Whole Grain Blend Pecan and Garlic
flavor.

Asian Cabbage Salad with Garlic Sesame Dressing

2   cups packaged shredded green cabbage

2   cups packaged shredded red cabbage

1   cup packaged shredded carrots

15 cherry or grape tomatoes, halved

1   (15-ounce) can hearts of palm, drained and sliced

1   (15-ounce) can Chinese baby corn, drained, cut into thirds

1   (8-ounce) can sliced water chestnuts, drained

For Dressing:

⅓   cup teriyaki sauce

⅓   cup olive oil

1   tablespoon toasted sesame oil

2   tablespoons sesame seeds

2   frozen cubes crushed garlic

1   teaspoon honey

1   teaspoon ground ginger or
    2 teaspoons fresh grated ginger

○ In a salad bowl, place cabbages, carrots, tomatoes, hearts of palm, baby corn and water chestnuts.

○ In a separate small bowl, whisk together all dressing ingredients. Pour dressing over salad. Toss lightly, just enough to coat.

○ Serve at room temperature or chill in refrigerator for 30 minutes.

Add some greens to the salad by tossing in 2 cups of baby spinach or mixed field greens just before serving.

85

Israeli Cabbage Salad

PREP: 4 minutes

COOK: none

CHILL: 1 hour

YIELD: 6 servings

1   (10-ounce) bag shredded red cabbage

4   tablespoons light mayonnaise

1   tablespoon fresh lemon juice

¼   teaspoon salt

¼   teaspoon pepper

○ Place cabbage, mayonnaise, lemon juice, salt and pepper in a salad bowl.

○ Mix to coat cabbage.

○ Chill for 1 hour and serve.

This was the first Israeli dish I made from scratch for the famous Chanie Geller Israeli salad course. It's so super easy that I make it all the time as a pretty and nourishing complement to any meal. My sister-in-law slices her own cabbage and that's how she instructed me to make the salad. But you know me. I found that the shredded, bagged cabbage is just as good. Trust me on this.

PREP: 5 minutes
COOK: none
CHILL: none
YIELD: 4 servings

Italian Tomato Salad

2   (10-ounce) boxes grape tomatoes,
      cut in half through stem end

For Dressing:

½   cup olive oil

2   tablespoons balsamic vinegar

2   tablespoons prepared minced garlic

2   teaspoons dried oregano

2   teaspoons basil

1   teaspoon kosher salt

½   teaspoon pepper

○ Place tomatoes in medium bowl.

○ In a small bowl, mix all dressing ingredients. Pour over tomatoes.

○ Toss and serve.

○ Mix red, yellow and orange grape tomatoes for a spectacular look and line the
   bowl with a few large red cabbage leaves
   for a gorgeous presentation.

Warm Pepper and Craisin Salad

PREP: 8 minutes
COOK: 5 minutes
CHILL: none
YIELD: 8 servings

3   tablespoons olive oil

1   red bell pepper, seeded, veins removed, diced

1   yellow bell pepper, seeded, veins removed, diced

1   green bell pepper, seeded, veins removed, diced

½   cup Craisins or dried cranberries

1   tablespoon balsamic vinegar

1   teaspoon salt

1   (8-ounce) package mixed field greens

For Dressing:

¼   cup mayonnaise

2   tablespoons balsamic vinegar

1   tablespoon Dijon-style mustard

1   tablespoon sugar

○ Heat olive oil in a 12-inch skillet over medium-high heat and sauté peppers for 1 to 2 minutes.

○ Add Craisins, balsamic vinegar and salt. Mix well.

○ Cover and cook over medium-low heat for about 5 minutes or until peppers are slightly tender.

○ While peppers are cooking, place all dressing ingredients in a food processor and pulse 3 or 4 times; alternatively, whisk together by hand. Process or whisk until smooth and creamy.

○ Place mixed field greens in a salad bowl. Pour dressing over and toss gently. Top with warm pepper mixture. Serve warm.

At Bistro Grill, our favorite neighborhood steakhouse in Woodmere, New York, Serge, the chef, makes a fabulous salad using smoked salmon, Craisins, pine nuts and red peppers, all dressed in balsamic vinaigrette. I've made that salad into two recipes. One is the Warm Salmon Salad (page 76) and one is this Warm Pepper and Craisin Salad. You'll find they are each flavorful enough to stand on their own.

PREP: 9 minutes

COOK: none

CHILL: none

YIELD: 6 to 8 servings

Crunchy Tofu Thai Salad

1   (8-ounce) package mixed field greens

½   cup chow mein noodles

½   cup slivered almonds

½   (14-ounce) package extra firm tofu, cut into bite-size pieces

For Dressing:

¾   teaspoon hot pepper sesame oil

2   tablespoons plain sesame oil

½   cup peanut butter

¼   cup soy sauce

1   tablespoon red wine vinegar

3   tablespoons rice vinegar

1   tablespoon brown sugar

1½ teaspoons prepared minced garlic

1   teaspoon ground ginger, or 2 teaspoons fresh grated ginger

½   teaspoon salt

- Place the field greens, noodles and almonds in a large salad bowl. Set aside.
- Place all dressing ingredients in a mini food processor or blender. Process until smooth. Pour into a medium bowl.
- Add tofu to dressing and toss well to coat.
- Spoon tofu and dressing over greens. Toss and serve.

For a warm salad, place tofu and dressing in a sealable plastic bag or container with a tight lid. Marinate for a minimum of 4 hours, then drain, reserving dressing. Sauté tofu in 2 tablespoons toasted sesame oil until warm and slightly crisp. Toss with greens and reserved dressing just before serving.

PREP: 8 minutes
COOK: 10 to 15 minutes
CHILL: 30 minutes
YIELD: 6 to 8 servings

Herb Seasoned Croutons

5   thick slices day-old bread (challah, white bread, sourdough or whole wheat), cubed

1   tablespoon dried oregano

1   tablespoon dried parsley flakes

1   tablespoon onion powder

1   tablespoon garlic powder

1   teaspoon kosher salt

½   cup olive oil

92

○ Preheat oven to 425° F.

○ Lightly grease two 9 x 13-inch pans with non-stick cooking spray.

○ Divide bread cubes evenly between prepared pans.

○ Sprinkle with oregano, parsley, onion and garlic powders, and salt.

○ Drizzle with olive oil.

○ Bake at 425° for 10 to 15 minutes, until light brown and crisp.

○ Allow croutons to cool at room temperature for 30 minutes and use to garnish salad.

Homemade croutons are always a big hit. Until I discovered how easy it is to make them, I used to omit croutons from all recipes that called for them. (The store-bought ones didn't appeal to me at all.) I love to make my croutons out of challah, which has a subtle hint of sweetness.

Croutons will last at least 2 weeks, if cravings can be controlled and they're stored properly. Once they are fully cooled, keep them in large, sealable plastic bags.

PREP: 10 minutes
COOK: none
CHILL: 1 hour
YIELD: 4 servings

Israeli Salad

2   Kirby or 3 Persian cucumbers, peeled and diced

1   red bell pepper, seeded, veins removed, diced

10 grape tomatoes, quartered, or 1 beefsteak tomato, diced

1   tablespoon fresh lemon juice

1   tablespoon olive oil

1   teaspoon dried parsley or 1 tablespoon fresh minced parsley

½   teaspoon salt

½   teaspoon black pepper

    Fresh cilantro or additional parsley, for garnish (optional)

○ Combine cucumbers, bell pepper, tomatoes, lemon juice, oil, parsley, salt and pepper in medium-sized salad bowl and mix well.

○ Chill for 1 hour.

○ Just before serving, garnish salad with fresh cilantro or parsley, if desired.

I used to buy Israeli salad all the time, because it's so good, so healthy for you and so refreshing. But I always felt guilty when I got to the checkout line, because it's so expensive. That was before I knew how easy it was to make it yourself. Now I just buy tomatoes, cucumbers and peppers, and return home with zero guilt!

No wonder this is the quintessential salad from Israel. Even though half of the country is desert, Israel has some amazing produce. Its oranges, mangos and tomatoes are among the finest in the world.

Colorful Garden Salad with Creamy Pesto Dressing

PREP: 12 minutes
COOK: none
CHILL: none
YIELD: 10 servings

2   romaine hearts, shredded about ¼-inch thick

½   yellow or orange bell pepper, seeded, veins removed, diced

½   red or green bell pepper, seeded, veins removed, diced

½   cup packaged shredded red cabbage

½   cup packaged shredded carrots

15   cherry or grape tomatoes, halved

½   cup canned white shoepeg corn or sweet yellow corn Niblets, drained

½   cup canned Chinese baby corn, drained

½   cup canned hearts of palm, drained and diced

1   large ripe Hass avocado, peeled, pitted and diced

2   Kirby or Persian cucumbers, peeled and sliced

½   cup croutons

For Dressing:

¼   cup liquid non-dairy creamer

¼   cup mayonnaise

¼   cup prepared pesto

1   teaspoon prepared crushed garlic

2   tablespoons pine nuts, plus more for garnish

1   teaspoon salt

○ Place lettuce, peppers, cabbage, carrots, tomatoes, corn, hearts of palm, avocado, cucumbers and croutons in a large salad bowl.

○ In a small bowl, whisk together all dressing ingredients until smooth and creamy.

○ Pour dressing over salad and toss lightly.

○ Garnish with additional pine nuts and serve.

○ This salad is exquisite when layered in a clear glass trifle bowl. Depending on the size and circumference of your bowl, you may have to double or triple some of the ingredients to complete an entire layer. Be sure to layer the lettuce in at least 2 if not 3 places. Serve dressing on the side.

Fish:
The Fight over Fish

I'll admit that when it comes to fish, Hubby and I don't see eye to eye. I can eat the stuff (along with my soups and salads) night and day. For him to go near fish, the moon and stars need to be aligned just right, the lights must be low and a few aperitifs don't hurt, either.

There is one fish recipe he does go for, though, and that's my friend Anita's Chilled Salmon with Dijon Dipping Sauce (page 37). I like to call it Secret Salmon Surprise because Hubby and I are always surprised that he enjoys it. The truth is, I don't think Anita invented the recipe. She probably saw it somewhere. Some people seem to absorb recipe ideas. My editor's friend loves to read cookbooks just for fun.

Such a pastime was once as foreign to me as going to a bull-fight, but I'm beginning to understand it now. Maybe someday I'll crack open all those gift cookbooks that are sitting on my shelf.

Anyway, chilled salmon is apparently the way to lure a man who "hates fish" to the table. We started with chilled salmon, and now, only two years later, he'll take a bite of grilled tuna if it's smothered in sauce. Around here, that's progress.

Hubby's biases notwithstanding, one of the first fish dishes I mastered was Crispy Rainbow Trout (page 111). My grand-father got the recipe from a woman on a porch in a remote mountain town in Transylvania. Sounds like a really monstrous old country recipe, the kind that takes weeks of nurturing, doesn't it? But there's nothing to it (really!), as you'll see in this chapter. The secret is the rainbow trout itself (even the name is gorgeous), and the wisdom behind this minimal recipe is to simply allow the natural taste of this succulent species to come through. I've since added crispy fried onions to the recipe because when you throw fried onions on almost any-thing, you can hook a finicky fish eater into trying it – and you know who I mean.

For tips on selecting, cooking and storing fish, read my interview with the fish department manager at Supersol supermarket on page 260.

Grouper with Pineapple and Corn Chutney

PREP: 6 minutes

COOK: 18 to 22 minutes

CHILL: none

YIELD: 6 servings

6   grouper fillets, about 3 pounds

½   teaspoon salt

½   teaspoon coarse black pepper

4   tablespoons olive oil

For Chutney:

2   tablespoons olive oil

1   (11-ounce) can sweet yellow corn Niblets, drained

1   (11-ounce) can white shoepeg corn, drained

¾   cup dried pineapple bits

¼   cup raisins

½   cup prepared chunky salsa, mild

○ Preheat broiler. Lightly grease a broiler pan with non-stick cooking spray.

○ Rinse grouper, pat dry and place in prepared pan.

○ Season with salt and pepper and drizzle with olive oil.

○ Broil for 5 to 7 minutes on each side.

○ To make chutney: In a 2-quart saucepan, heat olive oil over low heat. Add both kinds of corn, pineapple, raisins and salsa. Stir to mix.

○ Cover and simmer for 8 minutes. Remove from heat.

○ Place grouper on platter and spoon chutney on top. Serve immediately.

My best friend Rozanna came home from a restaurant raving about a chutney she had. Her mouthwatering description inspired this dish. The raisins and pineapple lend a delectable sweetness to the chutney.

If you have a hard time getting grouper, substitute tilefish, red snapper, flounder, striped bass or any other white-fleshed fish.

Suggested Wine: Hagafen 2005 Potter Valley White Riesling. Grouper needs a light white wine to set off the delicacy of its flesh, but the sweet and spicy sauce calls for a wine with a bit of pizzazz. Potter Valley Riesling it is!

PREP: 1 minute

COOK: 25 minutes

CHILL: none

YIELD: 6 servings

Black Bean and Salsa Salmon

6   salmon fillets, about 3 pounds

1   (16-ounce) jar prepared hot salsa

¼   cup canned black beans, drained

1   ripe Hass avocado, peeled, pitted
      and sliced (optional)

○ Preheat oven to 350° F. Lightly grease a
   9 x 13-inch pan with non-stick cooking
   spray.

○ Rinse salmon and pat dry. Place in prepared pan.

○ Mix salsa and black beans in a bowl and
   pour over salmon.

○ Bake, uncovered, at 350° for 25 minutes.

○ Garnish with sliced avocado, if desired.

Salmon is a big winner, cold or warm,
in terms of taste. Even among non-fish
eaters, salmon often goes over well.

Sesame Crusted Yellowfin Tuna with Wasabi Sauce

6   yellowfin tuna steaks, 2-inches thick, about 3 pounds

½   cup low-sodium soy sauce

4   tablespoons sesame oil

¼   cup sesame seeds

    Pickled ginger (optional)

For Sauce:

1   cup wasabi sauce

1   cup mayonnaise

½   cup Dijon-style mustard

- Preheat oven to 400° F. Lightly grease a 9 x 13-inch pan with non-stick cooking spray.

- Place soy sauce in deep bowl.

- Rinse tuna and pat dry. Dip in soy sauce.

- Remove tuna and place in prepared pan.

- Brush or drizzle with sesame oil and sprinkle with sesame seeds.

- Bake, uncovered, at 400° for 8 to 10 minutes for medium, or until desired doneness.

- Mix all sauce ingredients in a small bowl.

- Arrange tuna on individual plates and drizzle with about half the sauce. Serve remaining sauce on the side for dipping. Garnish with pickled ginger if desired.

Suggested Wine: Hagafen 2005 Potter Valley White Riesling.
This Riesling has a bit of residual sugar, which will complement the ginger, and its acid will contrast with the soy and wasabi really well. Rieslings and Asian food always work!

Yellowfin tuna gets its name from its long, bright yellow fins. The largest yellowfins can weigh more than 100 lbs and their high fat content makes them desirable. The rich, red flesh of the yellowfin cooks to a wonderful white "steak." Tuna is great for searing, broiling, baking and sautéing.

Chilean Sea Bass in Honeyed Pecan Sauce

6 Chilean sea bass fillets, about 3 pounds

½ cup candied pecans, chopped

½ cup low-sodium soy sauce

¼ cup honey

¼ cup light brown sugar, packed

2 tablespoons olive oil

Additional candied pecans, for garnish (optional)

○ Preheat oven to 350° F. Spray a 9 x 13-inch pan with non-stick cooking spray.

○ Rinse sea bass and pat dry. Place in prepared pan.

○ In a bowl, mix together pecans, soy sauce, honey, brown sugar and olive oil.

○ Spoon over sea bass.

○ Bake, uncovered, at 350° for 20 to 25 minutes. Garnish with a few whole candied pecans, if desired.

The candied pecans provide a pleasant contrast to the tender fish.

Mustard and Ginger Salmon

6   salmon fillets, about 3 pounds

1   (2-inch) piece ginger, peeled
     and chopped

4   tablespoons Dijon-style mustard

1   tablespoon prepared crushed garlic

3   tablespoons olive oil

½   teaspoon salt

¼   teaspoon pepper

○ Preheat oven to 425° F. Spray a 9 x 13-
   inch pan with non-stick cooking spray.

○ Rinse salmon and pat dry. Place in
   prepared pan.

○ In a small bowl, whisk together ginger,
   mustard, garlic, olive oil, salt and pepper
   until creamy. Pour over salmon.

○ Bake, uncovered, at 425° for 10 to 12
   minutes.

○ Arrange on individual plates and serve.

This is another original from my good
friend Monet. One night after work,
I went over for dinner and she had
made this salmon. I craved it for years
and finally had it again when we were
testing it for the cookbook. Double
the sauce and serve it on the side for
extra dipping.

Suggested Wine: Hagafen 2004 Oak Knoll District of Napa Valley
Chardonnay. Salmon needs a full-bodied wine to support its oily goodness. This Chardonnay will do that, and its hints of spice will nicely
complement the mustard and garlic in this sauce.

Seared Yellowfin Tuna Over White Beans

PREP: 9 minutes

COOK: 4 minutes

CHILL: none

YIELD: 6 servings

107

1½   teaspoons sea salt

1½   teaspoons garlic powder

½   teaspoon coarse black pepper

½   teaspoon cumin

½   teaspoon brown sugar

½   teaspoon dried basil

6   yellowfin tuna steaks, 2-inches thick, about 3 pounds

2   tablespoons canola oil

For Beans:

2   (15-ounce) cans white beans, rinsed and drained

¼   cup canola oil

1   tablespoon fresh lemon juice

⅛   teaspoon coarse black pepper

¼   teaspoon garlic powder

¼   cup chopped fresh parsley

○ In a small bowl, mix together salt, garlic powder, pepper, cumin, brown sugar and basil.

○ Rinse tuna and pat dry. Rub with spice mixture.

○ Heat oil in a 12-inch skillet over high heat. Add the tuna, being careful not to crowd.

○ Sauté 2 minutes on each side, until seared. Tuna should be cooked outside and still red inside. Set aside.

○ Place beans in a large bowl. Add oil, lemon juice, pepper, garlic powder and parsley. Stir gently to mix.

○ To serve, divide bean mixture among 6 plates and top each with a tuna steak.

Suggested Wine: Hagafen 2003 Estate Bottled Napa Valley Merlot. Think of seared tuna like meat and you'll know why Merlot has to be the one. Plus, the exotic spices in the wine will pair perfectly with the cumin and brown sugar.

○ Seared means still raw on the inside and you have to be into that sort of thing. Buy good quality tuna and you won't regret it.

Walnut Crusted Chilean Sea Bass with Lemon Dill Sauce

½ cup ground walnuts

1 cup bread crumbs

¼ teaspoon wasabi powder

1½ tablespoons Dijon-style mustard

1 tablespoon mayonnaise

6 Chilean sea bass fillets, about 3 pounds

Non-stick cooking spray

For Dressing:

¾ cup mayonnaise

3 tablespoons non-dairy creamer

1½ tablespoons fresh dill, chopped

2 teaspoons lemon juice

½ teaspoon prepared chopped garlic

½ teaspoon Dijon-style mustard

PREP: 9 minutes

COOK: 20 minutes

CHILL: none

YIELD: 6 servings

109

○ Preheat oven to 350° F. Lightly grease a 9 x 13-inch pan with non-stick cooking spray.

○ In a small bowl, mix together walnuts, bread crumbs, wasabi, mustard and mayonnaise and set aside.

○ Rinse sea bass and pat dry. Place in prepared pan.

○ Press nut mixture onto fillets.

○ Spray fillets with non-stick cooking spray.

○ Bake, uncovered, at 350° for 20 minutes.

○ In small bowl, mix together all dressing ingredients until well blended.

○ Serve sea bass with a drizzle of lemon-dill sauce with extra on the side for dipping.

Suggested Wine: Hagafen 2005 Napa Valley Sauvignon Blanc. The rich sauce in this recipe needs citrus to cut its impact on the tongue. This Sauvignon Blanc will do that in spades, and its nuances of spice will complement the mustard, too.

○ So chic, yet so easy! The ground walnuts make for an unexpected and crunchy topping. The lemon dill sauce provides a light balance to the bass, a meaty, fatty fish. Double or triple the sauce and use it as a dressing for a simple side salad.

Crispy Rainbow Trout

6   rainbow trout fillets, about
    3 pounds

1½ teaspoons salt

¾   teaspoon coarse black pepper

4½ teaspoons paprika

4   tablespoons olive oil

o Preheat broiler. Spray a broiler pan with
   non-stick cooking spray.

o Rinse trout and pat dry. Arrange fillets in
   prepared pan.

o Season with salt, pepper and paprika.
   Drizzle olive oil over fish.

o Broil for 5 minutes or until slightly brown
   and crispy at edges. Place trout on a
   platter and serve immediately.

111

This was my grandfather's recipe. We used to beg him for this delicacy every time we'd go to his house for lunch. One day I arrived early and actually caught him cooking his famous trout. I respect him for making something so simple. He figured out what you don't need to do – add too many ingredients to hide a good thing. "This is it?" I asked. It wasn't that the method was so complicated; it was that the fish was so fresh – possibly the best fish I had ever tasted.

At the time, as a child, it seemed to me that there should have been a lot of magic and secret ingredients.

But that *was* it.

For an added crunch, warm a can of fried onion rings in a skillet or in the oven for just a few minutes. Serve on top of or alongside the trout.

Salmon Casserole

PREP: 12 minutes

COOK: 45 minutes

CHILL: none

YIELD: 6 servings

1   green or red bell pepper, seeded,
    veins removed, diced

2   celery stalks, minced

1   large Vidalia onion, minced

2   (6-ounce) cans salmon, drained
    and mashed

2   cups mayonnaise

1½ teaspoons Worcestershire sauce

1½ cups seasoned bread crumbs,
    divided

½   teaspoon salt

¼   teaspoon coarse black pepper

○ Preheat oven to 350° F. Lightly spray a
2-quart baking dish with non-stick cooking spray.

○ In a large mixing bowl place bell pepper,
celery, onion, salmon, mayonnaise, Worcestershire sauce, 1 cup bread crumbs,
salt and pepper. Mix well.

○ Transfer mixture to prepared dish.

○ Sprinkle remaining ½ cup bread crumbs
on top.

○ Bake, uncovered, at 350° for 45 minutes.

○ Scoop out onto plates and serve.

My English professor once told our class
that as a young bride she took a post-
graduate course in medieval Spanish
literature. Arduously plugging her way,
chapter by chapter, through a cookbook
after classes, she put off selecting a subject for her term paper, hoping to come
up with something at the last minute.
To her dismay, one day her professor
went around the class, asking each person the subject of his or her upcoming
paper. When he pointed a bony finger
at her and asked, "And you, what are
you up to?" she truthfully answered
"Casseroles." "Casseroles," he repeated,
smiling, his eyes closed in concentration.
"Excellent! Excellent!" To this day, she
doesn't know if "casseroles" is an obscure
Spanish poet or if the professor was
bluffing!

Cod in a Light Lime Sauce

6   cod fillets, about 3 pounds

¼   teaspoon salt

¾   teaspoon butcher's cut cracked
      black pepper

4   tablespoons olive oil

1   lime, halved

      Brown rice, cooked according
      to package directions (optional)

○ Preheat oven to 425° F. Spray a 9 x 13-inch
   pan with non-stick cooking spray.

○ Rinse cod and pat dry. Place in prepared pan.

○ Sprinkle with salt and pepper. Drizzle with
   olive oil.

○ Squeeze juice of half a lime over fish. Cut
   remaining half into 4 thin slices. Place one
   slice over each piece of cod.

○ Bake, uncovered, at 425° for 20 minutes.

○ Serve with brown rice, if desired.

Suggested Wine: Hagafen 2005 Napa Valley Sauvignon Blanc
Just as the sauce will emphasize and add zing to the cod, the Sauvignon
Blanc will accent it because of its own citrusy essence.

○ Butcher's cut cracked black pepper is
an even coarser and larger-flaked spice
than coarse black pepper. It's beautiful
in contrast to the white flesh of the fish
and is especially appealing with the
lime slices.

Poultry:
Fuss and Feathers

As a former vegetarian, the food I resisted most was poultry, surprisingly more so than red meat. Granted, I had made up my mind that once married, I would cook and eat chicken, but I knew it would be an uphill climb. So I worked on it, telling myself that eating a piece of chicken was child's play.

To test my resolve during our engagement, we went to a very fancy meat restaurant. Perhaps I was a bit overconfident in my carnivorous cravings, because I boldly ordered a $30 piece of chicken (on the bone) and closed my menu with a smile. When the little chickie arrived, my soon-to-be-husband read me like a book. He quickly sent the poor thing back to the kitchen and ordered my usual, portobello mushroom salad.

Fast forward to my kitchen, a week into my marriage. I am staring at a dead chicken, wondering if there is a way to cook it without touching it. Hubby comes to my rescue, deftly walking me through the process, showing me in baby steps how to properly rinse a chicken (which is under cold running water), clean a chicken (which is to cut away any excess fat and or loose skin) and how to wield an 8-inch chef's knife.

After all the prep training, Hubby introduced me to his all-time favorite chicken recipe. Drum roll, please: duck sauce chicken. Yup, it's chicken with duck sauce just slathered over it. Now here was a "recipe" that was just my speed. I actually measured out the exact amount of sauce for the purposes of this book, but in reality I never measure, just eyeball and dump.

Duck sauce chicken was the real basis for the concept of this cookbook: fast and easy recipes for the novice (or busy) cook.

The prep time of 3 minutes for duck sauce chicken includes 2 minutes and 50 seconds to clean the bird. Otherwise, the recipe takes 10 seconds – and people love it!

They always ask me what's on the chicken and I answer,
"Duck sauce."
And they say, "What else?"
"Nothing."
"Just duck sauce?"
"Yes, just duck sauce."

It's almost embarrassing. But I've since discovered that many chicken recipes are quick, and I've shared some of my faves in this section. You'll find the cutest little chickies: Cornish hens (1 to 2 pounders) that can be served whole to each person. And we've got the big bird here as well: a turkey recipe you can double and serve to an army, or have enough for leftovers for turkey sandwiches the next day – and the next.

It's easy to get started. Just turn the page to see what the fuss and feathers are all about.

PREP: 15 minutes

COOK: 15 to 20 minutes

CHILL: none

YIELD: 4 to 6 servings

Teriyaki Chicken and Peppers

3   pounds boneless chicken breast cutlets, sliced into strips

1   (20-ounce) bottle teriyaki sauce

2   tablespoons honey

4   tablespoons olive oil, divided

1   red bell pepper, seeded, veins removed, sliced into thin strips

1   green bell pepper, seeded, veins removed, sliced into thin strips

2   tablespoons sesame seeds

○ Rinse cutlets and pat dry.

○ Place chicken in a sealable plastic bag with teriyaki sauce and honey, shake to coat and set aside.

○ In a large skillet, heat 2 tablespoons olive oil over medium-high heat and sauté peppers for 10 minutes, until tender.

○ While that's cooking, in another large skillet, heat remaining 2 tablespoons olive oil over medium-high heat and sauté chicken strips for 10 to 15 minutes until cooked through.

○ Add balance of marinade (whatever is left in sealable plastic bag) to peppers and heat thoroughly for about 5 minutes.

○ Combine peppers and chicken and sprinkle with sesame seeds before serving.

Suggested Wine: Hagafen 2005 Potter Valley White Riesling.
The teriyaki and honey in this sauce demand the one and only: a high-acid, slightly sweet Riesling, the 2005 Potter Valley, in fact!

To vary this dish, double the marinade and add 2 sliced onions and 1 carton of sliced mushrooms to peppers when sautéing.

Southern-Style Chicken

1   chicken, about 3½ pounds,
    cut into 8 pieces
1   tablespoon McCormick fried
    chicken seasoning
2   tablespoons light mayonnaise
1   tablespoon Dijon-style mustard
¾   cup seasoned bread crumbs
    Non-stick cooking spray

○ Preheat oven to 375° F. Spray a 9 x 13-
  inch pan with non-stick cooking spray.

○ Rinse chicken and pat dry. Pull off skin
  using a dry paper towel and place
  chicken in prepared pan.

○ Rub fried chicken seasoning into the
  chicken.

○ Mix mayonnaise and mustard to blend,
  and then spread over chicken, coating
  all surfaces.

○ Coat both sides of chicken with bread
  crumbs and arrange in prepared pan.

○ Liberally spray non-stick cooking spray
  over chicken.

○ Bake, uncovered, at 375° for 1 hour.
  Chicken should be nicely browned and
  crunchy. Serve immediately.

Suggested Wine: Hagafen 2005 Napa Valley Sauvignon Blanc.
Breading and mustard sauces require something to cut the fat on the
tongue. The citrus and acid of the 2005 Sauvignon Blanc fit the bill.

○ My mother, the most unlikely source,
gave me a great tip about how to remove
skin from chicken. She told me she saw
the butcher use dry paper towels to just
pull off the skin in one fell swoop. I've
been using it as a time-saver ever since.

○ Substitute 2 tablespoons olive oil for the
mayonnaise or just use 3 tablespoons
of olive oil or mayonnaise if you are not
quite the Dijon fan that I am.

Coca-Cola Chicken

PREP: 7 minutes

COOK: 1 hour, 15 to 30 minute

CHILL: none

YIELD: 4 servings

1   (10-ounce) bag chopped onions or 2 large onions, sliced

1   chicken, about $3\frac{1}{2}$ pounds, cut into 8 pieces

1   teaspoon garlic powder

$\frac{1}{2}$ cup Coca-Cola

$\frac{1}{2}$ cup ketchup

$\frac{1}{2}$ cup apricot jam

1   tablespoon soy sauce

○ Preheat oven to 375° F. Lightly grease a 9 x 13-inch pan with non-stick cooking spray.

○ Place onions in prepared pan.

○ Rinse chicken and pat dry; arrange on top of onions.

○ Season chicken with garlic powder.

○ In a medium bowl, place Coca-Cola, ketchup, apricot jam and soy sauce, and mix well.

○ Pour Coca-Cola mixture over chicken and bake, uncovered, at 375° for 1 hour and 15 minutes to 1 hour and 30 minutes. Serve warm.

I didn't know this was a standard recipe, known to cooks of many countries. I received it via my sister's friend, Jennie, all the way from Israel. I waited five years to get the precise measurements in this recipe, but it was worth it!

Duck Sauce Chicken

PREP: 3 minutes

COOK: 1 hour, 15 minutes

CHILL: none

YIELD: 4 servings

1   chicken, about 3½ pounds, cut into 8 pieces

1¼ cups Cantonese-style duck sauce (Sweet & Sour)

○ Preheat oven to 375° F. Spray a 9 x 13-inch pan with non-stick cooking spray.

○ Rinse chicken and pat dry. Arrange in prepared pan.

○ Pour duck sauce liberally and evenly all over chicken.

○ Bake, uncovered, at 375° for 1 hour and 15 minutes, or until skin is crispy and brown. Chicken should look slightly blackened and barbecued.

○ This is the famous Duck Sauce Chicken I told you about in the introduction to this chapter. It was the first chicken dish I learned how to cook, under the tutelage of that great chef I married. This is undoubtedly my hubby's favorite chicken. Although I've spent hours mastering fancier poultry dishes, somehow we always come back to good ol' Duck Sauce Chicken. If it weren't so quick and easy, Hubby would have to find a new favorite.

Suggested Wine: Hagafen 2005 Potter Valley White Riesling.
Duck sauce is sweet with a tiny kick – so is this Potter Valley Riesling, and its high acid will guarantee a terrific match for this Chinese-inspired chicken dish.

Cold Poached Spinach and Walnut Pesto Chicken

6   boneless chicken breast cutlets, about 3 pounds
2   (10.5-ounce) cans condensed chicken broth
2½   cups water

For Sauce:

1   cup walnuts
2   cups baby spinach leaves
¾   cup basil leaves
4   cloves garlic, peeled and halved
½   teaspoon salt
¼   teaspoon black pepper
½   cup olive oil

PREP: 13 minutes
COOK: 35 minutes
CHILL: 1 hour
YIELD: 6 servings

125

○ Rinse cutlets and pat dry.

○ In a medium pot, bring chicken broth and water to a boil. Add chicken, and when the broth comes back to a boil, reduce to a simmer.

○ Cover and simmer for 15 minutes. Turn off heat and allow chicken to finish cooking from the retained heat for 15 minutes. Remove chicken from broth, cover and chill in refrigerator for 1 hour.

○ To prepare sauce, in a food processor or blender, place walnuts, spinach, basil, garlic, salt and pepper. Pulse 3 or 4 times. Pour the olive oil in a steady stream through feed tube while machine is running, until mixture is smooth and creamy, about 1 minute.

○ Spread pesto over cooled cutlets or cut cooled chicken into slices, and drizzle with pesto. Serve any additional sauce on the side.

Suggested Wine: Hagafen 2005 Napa Valley Sauvignon Blanc. Sauvignon Blanc has a hint of grassiness to it, a characteristic of its varietal nature that, along with its sweet citrus fruits, goes perfectly with the spinach, basil and walnuts.

○ Sautéing and browning the walnuts will release a bit more flavor. Place them in a skillet with 1 teaspoon canola oil over high heat for a minute or two. When warm and golden brown in color, proceed with Step 4.

PREP: 7 minutes

COOK: 1 hour, 25 minutes

CHILL: none

YIELD: 4 servings

Roasted Garlic Chicken and Baby Vegetables

1	chicken, about 3 ½ pounds, cut into 8 pieces
20	small fingerling potatoes or 10 large fingerling potatoes, halved
10	baby carrots
10	baby zucchini
10	baby red bell peppers
¾	cup olive oil
2	tablespoons prepared crushed garlic
1	tablespoon paprika
1	tablespoon garlic powder
½	teaspoon kosher salt

○ Preheat oven to 375° F. Spray a roasting pan with non-stick cooking spray.

○ Rinse chicken and pat dry. Arrange in prepared pan.

○ Rinse potatoes, carrots, zucchini and peppers and place in a medium bowl. Add oil, garlic, paprika, garlic powder and salt. Stir to mix.

○ Spoon vegetable mixture into the roasting pan, arranging the vegetables under and around chicken. Make sure chicken skin is coated with oil mixture. Pour any extra from the bowl to cover the skin.

○ Bake, uncovered, at 375° for 1 hour and 25 minutes, or until skin is slightly browned and crispy. Serve immediately.

You can use other seasonal mini vegetables – the smaller, the better. Gourmet restaurants serve 'em but anyone can. I find myself forgetting about the chicken and just eating these deliciously cute veggies by the spoonful!

Apricot Chicken

PREP: 8 minutes
COOK: 1 hour
CHILL: none
YIELD: 4 servings

1   chicken, about 3 ½ pounds, cut into 8 pieces
1½   teaspoons ground nutmeg
1   cup dried apricots, halved
½   cup apricot preserves
½   cup bottled Russian dressing
¼   cup duck sauce
2   tablespoons Osem Onion Soup Mix

○ Preheat oven to 375° F. Spray a 9 x 13-inch pan with non-stick cooking spray.

○ Rinse chicken and pat dry. Arrange in prepared pan.

○ Sprinkle with nutmeg.

○ In a small bowl, stir together apricots, preserves, Russian dressing, duck sauce and onion soup mix. Pour over chicken.

○ Bake, uncovered, at 375° for 1 hour. Skin should be crisp and brown. Serve immediately.

Apricots and chicken were really made to be cooked together. This is quite a standard recipe, though I find that every chef has their own variation. This one's a great starter for Apricot Chicken fans.

For an attractive garnish, add a few cinnamon sticks before serving. If you are lucky enough to find fresh, ripe apricots, pit and slice a few. Place over chicken before serving.

Baked Oniony Chicken

¼   cup olive oil

3   tablespoons Osem Onion Soup Mix, divided

3   large onions, thinly sliced

1   chicken, about 3½ pounds, cut into 8 pieces

1   tablespoon paprika

1   teaspoon coarse black pepper

○ Preheat oven to 375° F. Lightly grease a 9 x 13-inch pan with non-stick cooking spray.

○ In a medium bowl, mix olive oil, 1 table-spoon onion soup mix, and onions.

○ Place about a quarter of the onion mixture on the bottom of prepared pan.

○ Rinse chicken pieces, pat dry and place on top of onions in pan.

○ Season chicken with remaining 2 table-spoons of onion soup mix, paprika and pepper.

○ Scatter remaining onion mixture on and around chicken, making sure to drizzle some of the remaining oil over chicken skin.

○ Bake, uncovered, at 375° for 1 hour or until chicken is browned.

My friend Malki told me all about her "easiest ever" family favorite: onion soup mix chicken. I just had to try it. She literally uses just onion soup mix, but I've added a few other steps and adapted it to indulge my baked onion cravings.

If you have enough time, slice an additional onion and stuff a few slivers under the skin of each piece of chicken.

Suggested Wine: Hagafen 2003 Estate Bottled Napa Valley Merlot. Baked chicken with spices will pair nicely with the 2003 Merlot because of its bergamot and black licorice – lots of zing to encourage another bite of chicken!

Speedy
Coq Au Vin

1	chicken, about 3½ pounds, cut into 8 pieces
8	small white onions, peeled
16	small white mushrooms, cleaned
¾	cup dry red wine
1	tablespoon fresh minced parsley
2	teaspoons crumbled dried thyme or 4 teaspoons fresh minced thyme
½	teaspoon coarse black pepper
⅔	cup margarine, melted
2	dried bay leaves

○ Preheat oven to 375° F. Spray a 9 x 13-inch pan with non-stick cooking spray.

○ Rinse chicken and pat dry. Place in prepared pan.

○ Arrange onions and mushrooms around the chicken. Pour wine over chicken and vegetables.

○ Sprinkle with parsley, thyme and pepper.

○ Drizzle melted margarine over chicken.

○ Tuck bay leaves into wine mixture at each side of the chicken.

○ Bake, uncovered, at 375° for 1 hour and 15 minutes, and serve immediately.

To save her newly married son from starvation, my mother-in-law, Karen, showed up one day and tactfully suggested that she and I cook a few things together. It's a good thing she did, too. This was the first dish we tried. Her version was a huge hit, but took triple the time that this one did. Now that I've adapted her recipe with my shortcuts, I don't have to cringe every time my husband requests the dish. I'm grateful to her for this, and her many kindnesses over the years.

●

Suggested Wine: Hagafen 2004 Estate Bottled Napa Valley Pinot Noir.
As the chicken cooks in the wine, it will take on savory layers of flavor. The 2004 Pinot Noir works so well here because of its notes of black fruits and toasted cocoa. For added matching, use this wine when preparing the dish.

Chicken Cacciatore

6   boneless chicken breast cutlets,
       about 3 pounds

2   teaspoons paprika

2   teaspoons onion powder

$^1/_2$ teaspoon black pepper

3   medium onions, chopped

3   cups prepared marinara sauce

$^3/_4$ cup green olives, pitted and sliced
       Spaghetti, cooked according to
       package directions (optional)

○ Preheat oven to 350° F. Lightly grease
  a 9 x 13-inch pan with non-stick cooking spray.

○ Rinse chicken cutlets, pat dry and place
  in prepared pan.

○ Season with paprika, onion powder and
  pepper.

○ Place onions over cutlets.

○ In a medium bowl, mix marinara and olives,
  and pour over chicken.

○ Bake, uncovered, at 350° for 25 to 35
  minutes, until no longer pink when sliced
  with a knife, but still juicy.

○ Serve over spaghetti, if desired.

Sautéing the onions first in olive oil
over medium heat for a few minutes
will release their flavor.

Suggested Wine: Hagafen 2004 Napa Valley Zinfandel.
Spicy tomatoes mean the slightly sweet and definitely spicy 2004 Zinfandel.

Roasted Cornish Hens with Finger-ling Potatoes

PREP: 8 minutes
COOK: 1 hour, 30 minutes
CHILL: none
YIELD: 4 servings

4   Cornish hens, about 1 to 2 pounds each

4   tablespoons prepared crushed garlic

1   teaspoon dried ground sage

1½ teaspoons dried ground rosemary

1   tablespoon paprika

1   tablespoon kosher salt

1½ teaspoons coarse black pepper

½   cup olive oil

20 fingerling potatoes

5   fresh basil leaves, snipped

- Preheat oven to 375° F.
- Rinse Cornish hens, pat dry and place in a 12 x 17-inch roasting pan.
- Spoon garlic under skin of hens and distribute evenly.
- Season hens with sage, rosemary, paprika, salt and pepper, rubbing some of the seasoning underneath the skin.
- Drizzle olive oil on hens.
- Bake, uncovered, at 375° for 40 minutes. Remove pan from oven and place potatoes around the hens. Return to oven and bake for 50 minutes, or until chicken is crispy and brown.
- Scatter fresh basil leaves over chicken and potatoes before serving.

People love getting one tiny bird apiece, along with the darling little fingerling potatoes. When I cook with them, I feel like a gourmet chef.

Cornish hens can be dry, so you may want to baste them with pan drippings occasionally.

Suggested Wine: Hagafen 2004 Oak Knoll District of Napa Valley Chardonnay. The apricot and honey of this Chardonnay will work quite well with the roasted skin of the game hens, and the slight creaminess of the wine will accent the potatoes.

Arroz con Pollo

PREP: 10 minutes
COOK: 1 hour, 20 minutes
CHILL: none
YIELD: 4 servings

2 tablespoons olive oil

1 large onion, chopped or 1 (10-ounce) bag frozen chopped onions

1 red bell pepper, seeded, veins removed, diced

1 (8-ounce) carton sliced mushrooms

2 (5.6-ounce) boxes Near East Spanish Rice

2½ cups water

1 chicken, about 3½ pounds, cut into 8 pieces

1 teaspoon turmeric

1 teaspoon garlic powder

1 teaspoon paprika

Tortilla chips (optional)

- Preheat oven to 375° F. Spray a 9 x 13-inch pan with non-stick cooking spray.

- Heat oil in a 12-inch skillet over medium heat. Add onions, pepper and mushrooms and sauté for 5 minutes.

- Transfer vegetables to prepared pan. Add Spanish rice, including enclosed spice packets and water. Stir to mix.

- Rinse chicken, pat dry and place over rice.

- Sprinkle chicken with turmeric, garlic powder and paprika.

- Bake, uncovered, at 375° for 1 hour and 20 minutes, until chicken is golden brown. Serve with tortilla chips on the side, if desired.

Another original from my recipe tester, Joy, and very much in keeping with her California cooking style. We thought it was a perfect match for the Near East Spanish Rice. I once made the rice alone as a quickie side dish for a friend and she just had to know my "secret" recipe. I was a little embarrassed to tell her it came straight from a box!

Suggested Wine: Hagafen 2001 Estate Bottled Napa Valley Syrah. Spicy Arroz con Pollo wants a spicy wine by its side. The leather and tannins of this 2001 Syrah will balance against the peppers, mushrooms and paprika.

137

Honey Chicken

1	chicken, about 3 ½ pounds, cut into 8 pieces
¾	cup honey
¼	cup soy sauce
¼	cup olive oil
1	tablespoon garlic powder
1	teaspoon black pepper

- Preheat oven to 375° F. Lightly grease a 9 x 13-inch pan with non-stick cooking spray.
- Rinse chicken, pat dry and place in prepared pan.
- In a small bowl, mix together honey, soy sauce, olive oil, garlic powder and pepper and pour over chicken.
- Bake, uncovered, at 375° for 1 hour until slightly browned.

Suggested Wine: Hagafen 2004 Estate Bottled Napa Valley Pinot Noir.
The mix of savory and sweet in this dish calls for a wine of good body and complementary flavors. The spicy jam flavors of this Pinot will match wonderfully.

Despite its name, this chicken is not too sweet. The olive oil, soy sauce, garlic and pepper temper the honey perfectly.

Turkey Loaf

½   cup boiling water mixed with 1 ½
    tablespoons Osem Consommé Mix

1   (16-ounce) package chopped frozen
    spinach, thawed and drained

3   eggs, lightly beaten

3 ½ pounds ground turkey breast

½   cup dried minced onion flakes

2   tablespoons olive oil

½   teaspoon crumbled dried thyme

⅓   cup Worcestershire sauce

1   cup bread crumbs

2   teaspoons sea salt

1   teaspoon coarse black pepper

○ Preheat oven to 350° F. Liberally spray two
  9 x 5 x 3-inch loaf pans with non-stick
  cooking spray.

○ In a large bowl, mix consommé broth, spinach, eggs, turkey, onion flakes, olive oil,
  thyme, Worcestershire, bread crumbs,
  salt and pepper, until combined. Do not
  over mix.

○ Place mixture in prepared loaf pans. Smooth
  top with the back of a spoon.

○ Bake, uncovered, at 350° for 1 hour and
  30 minutes.

○ Drain off any excess juices. Strain and save.

○ Slice and arrange on serving platter. Pour
  saved juices over turkey loaf and serve hot
  or cold.

○ Using Worcestershire sauce in a kosher
kitchen can be tricky, because it contains
anchovies. Check the kosher certification mark. When it is accompanied
by a "fish" notation, it means that the
level of anchovies is greater than 1.6%
of the whole product. When the kosher
certification mark stands alone, the
percentage of anchovies is less than
1.6%. When using Worcestershire
sauce with meat dishes, use a brand
with a stand-alone kosher certification.

○ For added flavor, spread a topping over
each loaf during the last 45 minutes of
baking. Use ½ cup of ketchup for one
loaf, and create a Dijonnaise topping
for the other by combining ¼ cup light
mayo, ¼ cup Dijon-style mustard and
1 teaspoon lemon juice.

Cranberry Chicken

PREP: 5 minutes
COOK: 50 to 55 minutes
CHILL: none
YIELD: 4 to 6 servings

½ cup flour

¾ cup orange juice

2 cups fresh or frozen cranberries

1 cup sugar

¼ cup margarine

¼ teaspoon cinnamon

¼ teaspoon nutmeg

¼ teaspoon ginger

1 teaspoon salt

6 boneless chicken breast cutlets, about 3 pounds

- In a small saucepan, over medium heat, blend flour with orange juice, adding juice slowly, whisking to keep smooth.

- Add cranberries, sugar, margarine, cinnamon, nutmeg, ginger and salt. Stir to mix.

- Bring to a boil, stirring constantly to avoid lumps.

- Cool cranberry mixture slightly.

- Rinse cutlets and pat dry. Place in a large, deep skillet.

- Pour cranberry mixture over chicken in skillet.

- Cover and simmer 40 minutes. Serve immediately.

This dish is so delicious that you can eat it cold, straight from the fridge. I've even been known to sneak back into the kitchen to enjoy an extra helping as a sweet post-dessert bite. (Hey, I was pregnant, all right?)

Suggested Wine: Hagafen 2005 Potter Valley White Riesling.
The Potter Valley Riesling's good acid and exotic fruits – peach, apricot, mango and papaya – will beautifully pull together the varied flavors in this dish.

Hot and Spicy Turkey Wings

PREP: 3 minutes

COOK: 2 hours

CHILL: none

YIELD: 4 to 6 servings

4   turkey wings, about $^3/_4$ pound each, split

4   tablespoons McCormick's Montreal chicken seasoning

- Preheat oven to 375° F. Spray a 9 x 13-inch pan with non-stick cooking spray.

- Rinse turkey wings and pat dry. Sprinkle both sides liberally with seasoning and place in prepared pan.

- Bake, uncovered, at 375° for 2 hours. Serve warm.

Our Uncle, our lawyer, our friend Morse gave us this foolproof recipe. He must have anticipated his new niece's cooking skills with this winner. But like all Geller men, he happens to be a wiz in the kitchen – and not just with cooking. He carves a beautiful turkey, slices a delish brisket and even does dishes. When I saw him in the kitchen just as much as his wife Judi, I knew I wanted to marry into this family.

For a super duper spicy wing, after 1 hour, drain and turn the wings over. Sprinkle again with the seasoning and a dash of chili powder, and continue to bake for 1 more hour.

Roasted Turkey

1 turkey, about 10 pounds

1 lemon, halved

6 sprigs fresh thyme

3 garlic cloves, peeled and smashed

3 large onions, peeled and quartered; divided

1 tablespoon paprika

1 tablespoon kosher salt

1 tablespoon coarse black pepper

4 tablespoons margarine

1/3 cup olive oil

PREP: 10 minutes

COOK: 2 hours, 30 minutes
(15 minutes per pound)

CHILL: none

YIELD: 8 to 10 servings

○ Preheat oven to 350° F. Lightly spray a 12 x 17-inch roasting pan with non-stick cooking spray.

○ Rinse turkey inside and out under cold running water. Pat dry.

○ Place turkey in prepared pan.

○ Stuff cavity of turkey with lemon, thyme, garlic and 1 of the onions.

○ In a bowl combine paprika, salt, pepper, margarine and olive oil. Microwave on high for about 20 to 30 seconds or until margarine has melted. Mix well.

○ Baste and rub the mixture on the turkey and under the skin.

○ Scatter the other 2 onions around the bottom of the pan. Loosely cover turkey with aluminum foil.

○ Bake, loosely covered, at 350° for 2 hours and 30 minutes (15 minutes per pound for turkeys less than 12 pounds and 12 minutes per pound for turkeys larger than 12 pounds), basting occasionally. The turkey is done when an instant-read digital meat thermometer inserted into the inner thigh reads 180° F to 185° F, or when the juices run clear when a long-tined fork is inserted into the thickest part of the inner thigh.

○ For golden and crisp skin, remove foil for last 45 minutes of baking. For neater slicing, let turkey stand for 20 minutes before carving.

○ During the last hour of baking, surround the turkey with 20 baby carrots; 3 sweet potatoes, sliced; 20 red bliss potatoes, halved; and 3 large heads of fennel, quartered. Sprinkle vegetables with kosher salt and pour 2 cups water over them.

Meat:
For Meat and Potatoes Men

You've heard so much about my mother that you may be wondering where my dad fits into my Grand Culinary Experiment. Actually, when it comes to the kitchen, my father is more at home than the rest of us. The cooking gene runs deep in his family, inherited from both of his parents. He has me convinced that in the old country, where recipes didn't exist, everyone instinctively knew the secrets continental chefs use to win blue ribbons.

Like many seasoned cooks, Daddy doesn't measure, he doesn't count. Asking him to explain his magic is like asking a physics professor to teach kindergarten. I don't speak his culinary language, but I do understand the mouth-watering impact of his specialties. I still remember him drying and hanging his own kielbasa from the rafters of our basement. He used to put me on his shoulders to pluck them down. Until just a few years ago, I actually thought they grew there – some sort of meat indigenous to Philly basement ceilings.

So I grew up thinking it was totally normal for men to be not only the breadwinners of a household, but the bread toasters as well. When my husband-to-be and I were dating, he told me all about how his father began the Geller tradition of working in the catering field some 40 years ago. The Geller boys, including my husband, his uncles and brothers all followed suit and did time in the kitchen. Needless to say, they can work wonders with a pot and a pilot light.

How cool, I thought. My dad shopped, my dad cooked, my husband shops, my husband cooks: This whole marriage thing will work out just great! But something inside told me that I had better learn the craft. So I tried to cook Hubby's favorite recipes. Tried and failed. But during our first year, the few times

I managed to master a family recipe, I saw just how delighted and thankful he was. Whoever said "the way to a man's heart is through his stomach" was dead on. I wouldn't say that it's the only way, but it's definitely one of the few essential paths.

Now I know that there are plenty of men, as well as women, reading this book. These days it's important for a guy to know his way around the kitchen. Maybe you're single and sick of eating out. Maybe you're married and your wife is busy with the kids, or starting her business empire. Clearly, it's up to you to put dinner on the table. It's going to be easier than you think. You can pick up this book and make a meal in a jiffy.

I've found that it's true that most men crave meat and potatoes. In this chapter you'll discover lots of terrific recipes destined to become staples in your family and sure to satisfy every one of your meat 'n' potatoes men.

For tips on selecting the right cut of meat for every purpose and price range, read my interview with the meat department manager at Supersol supermarket on page 256.

Pepper Steak

2 pounds pepper steak strips
1 tablespoon cornstarch
2 tablespoons cold water
3 tablespoons honey
3 tablespoons olive oil, divided
1 tablespoon prepared crushed garlic
½ teaspoon ginger
¼ cup soy sauce
1 green bell pepper, seeded,
veins removed, thinly sliced
1 red bell pepper, seeded,
veins removed, thinly sliced
2 large onions, thinly sliced
Jasmine rice, prepared according
to package directions (optional)

- Rinse pepper steak, pat dry and place in a large bowl.

- In a small bowl, blend cornstarch with cold water until smooth. Pour over steak.

- Add honey, 2 tablespoons olive oil, garlic, ginger and soy sauce. Stir to mix. Set aside.

- Heat the remaining 1 tablespoon olive oil in a medium skillet over high heat. Add peppers and onions and sauté for 3 minutes.

- Reduce heat to medium, cook 10 to 15 minutes longer or until vegetables are softened.

- In a large skillet, over high heat, sauté steak and honey mixture for 3 minutes. Reduce heat to medium, cover, and cook 10 to 15 minutes longer or until beef is cooked through.

- In a large serving bowl, combine peppers and onions with steak and mix. Serve warm with Jasmine rice, if desired.

PREP: 9 minutes
COOK: 20 to 25 minutes
CHILL: none
YIELD: 4 servings

147

Suggested Wine: Hagafen 2001 Estate Bottled Napa Valley Syrah.
Spicy Syrah will work wonders to pair with the peppers, ginger and soy of this dish.

Sweet and Pungent Asian Roast

PREP: 9 minutes

COOK: 2 hours to
2 hours, 30 minutes

CHILL: none

YIELD: 8 servings

1 (5-pound) top chuck French roast or silver tip roast

¼ cup soy sauce

¼ cup sesame oil

¼ cup olive oil

¼ cup teriyaki sauce

¼ cup honey

¼ cup Szechuan-style duck sauce (hot & spicy)

2 tablespoons ume plum vinegar

¼ cup prepared crushed garlic

¼ cup dried parsley flakes

○ Preheat oven to 325° F. Lightly grease a roasting pan with non-stick cooking spray.

○ Rinse roast, pat dry and place in prepared pan.

○ In a bowl, place soy sauce, sesame and olive oils, teriyaki sauce, honey, duck sauce, plum vinegar, garlic and parsley flakes. Stir to mix well. Pour over roast.

○ Cover pan with aluminum foil, sealing at the edges but tenting the foil so that it does not touch the roast.

○ Bake at 325° for 2 hours to 2 hours and 30 minutes until very tender.

○ Let stand at room temperature for 5 to 10 minutes before slicing diagonally against the grain.

Suggested Wine: Hagafen 2004 Estate Bottled Napa Valley Pinot Noir. Meat and Pinot are always friends, and the honey, soy, teriyaki and duck sauces in this recipe need a wine with exotic spices. This Pinot Noir's berries and licorice fit the bill.

Slicing diagonally against the grain means slicing at a slight angle, not straight down; cutting the roast this way with a sharp carving knife will help keep meat tender. Allowing it to cool slightly first keeps it from shredding and falling apart as you slice.

Chili

PREP: 10 minutes

COOK: 3 hours, 10 minutes

CHILL: none

YIELD: 8 to 10 servings

3   tablespoons olive oil

2   large onions, diced or 1 (10-ounce) bag frozen chopped onions

4   cloves garlic, peeled, minced or 4 frozen crushed garlic cubes

2   pounds ground beef

2   red bell peppers, seeded, veins removed, chopped

1   (20-ounce) can diced tomatoes, drained, reserve liquid

1   (6-ounce) can tomato paste

4   tablespoons chili powder

2   teaspoons crushed cumin seeds

2   teaspoons salt

³/₄   teaspoon cayenne pepper, or to taste

2   (15-ounce) cans kidney beans, drained and rinsed

○ Heat oil in a 6-quart stockpot over medium heat. Add onions and garlic and sauté for 2 minutes.

○ Add beef. Stir and cook until beef has lost most of its pinkness. Pour off fat.

○ Add bell peppers and tomatoes. Stir to mix.

○ Add enough water to reserved tomato liquid to equal 2¹/₂ cups. Stir into beef mixture.

○ Add tomato paste, chili powder, cumin, salt and cayenne pepper.

○ Bring to a boil, and then reduce heat and simmer, covered, for 3 hours.

○ Stir in beans just before serving. Heat through. Serve hot.

When my recipe tester, Joy, tried this at home, her son saw the chili and said, "Let's make chili dogs!" We thought it was a great idea. My husband would climb a spiked wall for a good chili dog. Now that I know how to prepare this, I can give him a delicious one at home. Boil or grill the hot dogs, place them in buns and ladle a few spoonfuls of chili over top.

Stuffed Peppers

2   tablespoons olive oil or canola oil

1   pound ground beef

2   teaspoons Worcestershire sauce *(see note, p. 139)*

½   teaspoon garlic powder

¼   teaspoon chili powder

2   tablespoons dried minced onion flakes

1   tablespoon dried parsley flakes

½   teaspoon black pepper

1   cup quick-cooking rice, prepared according to package directions

3½   cups prepared marinara sauce, divided

5   large red or green bell peppers, seeded, veins removed, tops cut off

○ Preheat oven to 350° F.

○ Heat oil in a large skillet over medium-high heat and sauté ground beef for 3 to 4 minutes, until it loses most of its pinkness. Pour off fat.

○ Add Worcestershire sauce, garlic and chili powders, onion flakes, parsley and black pepper and cook for 1 to 2 minutes, stirring continuously.

○ Mix in cooked rice and 2 cups of the marinara sauce until well combined.

○ Lightly stuff each pepper with beef and rice mixture and stand stuffed peppers upright in an ungreased 9 x 13-inch pan. Peppers should be standing upright and close together.

○ Pour remaining 1½ cups marinara sauce over top and around peppers.

○ Bake, uncovered, at 350° for 1 hour or until peppers are soft.

○ Spoon any remaining sauce from the pan over peppers before serving.

PREP: 8 minutes

COOK: 1 hour, 15 minutes

CHILL: none

YIELD: 5 servings

Garnish the stuffed peppers with their tops. You can create a more colorful platter by using a combination of green, red, yellow and orange peppers.

Brisket in
Wine Sauce

PREP: 9 minutes
COOK: 3 hours
CHILL: none
YIELD: 8 servings

1   (2½-pound) beef brisket, thick-cut
1   tablespoon paprika
½   teaspoon basil
1   teaspoon salt
1   teaspoon pepper
3   medium onions, sliced
2   cloves garlic, peeled, halved
1½   cups ketchup
1½   cups dry red wine
1½   cups water

○ Preheat oven to 325° F.

○ Rinse brisket. Place in roasting pan.

○ Rub paprika, basil, salt and pepper into meat.

○ Scatter onions and garlic over meat.

○ In a medium bowl, mix ketchup, wine and water. Pour over brisket.

○ Cover pan tightly with aluminum foil, tenting so that the foil does not touch the meat.

○ Bake at 325° for 3 hours, or until an instant-read digital meat thermometer inserted into the center of the brisket reads 190° for well done.

○ Let stand 5 to 10 minutes before slicing diagonally, against the grain. Serve warm, and pass pan juices in a sauce boat.

Suggested Wine: Hagafen 2001 Estate Bottled Napa Valley Syrah. The leather and licorice of the 2001 Syrah will match beautifully with the spicy yet sweet ketchup, the basil and the paprika in this sauce.

Sweet and Tangy Veal Chops

1   red bell pepper, seeded,
     veins removed, thinly sliced

1   medium green zucchini, thinly sliced

1   large onion, thinly sliced

6   (1-inch thick) veal chops

$\frac{1}{2}$ cup Szechuan-style duck sauce
     (hot & spicy)

$\frac{1}{4}$ cup low-sodium soy sauce

3   tablespoons Dijon-style mustard

○ Preheat broiler. Lightly grease a broiler pan with non-stick cooking spray.

○ Place pepper, zucchini and onion in prepared pan.

○ Rinse veal, pat dry, and place on top of vegetables.

○ In a bowl, mix duck sauce, soy sauce and mustard. Brush chops with sauce mixture.

○ Cook under preheated broiler for 10 to 12 minutes.

○ Flip chops and brush sauce on other side.

○ Broil for 8 to 10 minutes longer for well done. Let rest at least 5 minutes before serving.

My neighbors Devorah and Motty were not only champion taste testers for this book, but also donated a few of the recipes. One day, when we were walking our daughters in their carriages, Devorah said to me, "You'll never believe the most delicious and easy dinner I made for Motty last night!" I remember exactly what corner we stopped at, as she described this mouth-watering recipe. It's great when people want to share their kitchen secrets with you! I've heard there's a type of cook who won't give out recipes. Thankfully, I haven't run into one yet.

Suggested Wine: Hagafen 2004 Estate Bottled Napa Valley Pinot Noir. Given the wide range of flavors packed into this dish, only the most marvelous of food wines, Pinot Noir, will work to bring together these elements into a harmonious whole.

Standing Rib Roast

1   (10-pound) standing rib roast
        with 4 rib bones, meat separated
        from bones
1¼   cup soy sauce
1¼   cup light brown sugar, packed
½   cup honey
½   cup prepared crushed garlic
4   large onions, sliced

○ Preheat oven to 350° F. Rinse roast and
pat dry.

○ Place roast in a roasting pan, bone side
down, fat side up.

○ In a bowl, mix soy sauce, brown sugar,
honey and garlic. Pour the soy sauce
mixture all over the roast. Scatter onions
over and around the roast.

○ Bake, uncovered, at 350° for 2 hours,
or until an instant-read digital meat thermometer inserted into the center of the
roast reads 125° for medium rare, or 135°
for medium.

○ Let stand at room temperature for 15 to
20 minutes. Remove meat from bone
cradle and place rib side down to carve
large slices off the roast.

Suggested Wine: Hagafen 2002 Estate Bottled Napa Valley Cabernet
Sauvignon. Since roast beef is the king of meat dishes, the king of wines
is its natural pair. The Cabernet's black licorice and cherries, plus its full
body, will work perfectly here.

155

The standing rib roast is the king of beef
roasts, as it is usually large and costly.
A great piece of meat like this requires
nothing more than an impeccable bottle of wine for a true gourmet dining
experience.

Have your butcher do all the hard work
for you. Request that he separate the
meat from the rib bones and then tie the
meat back onto the bone cradle with
string. This will allow the bones to keep
the meat moist and flavorful, but will
make carving a walk in the park.

Teriyaki Skirt Steak

2½ pounds skirt or flank steak

1 cup teriyaki sauce

2 tablespoons canola oil

1 medium onion, chopped

1 (8-ounce) carton sliced mushrooms

White rice (optional)

○ Preheat oven to 450° F. Lightly grease a roasting pan with non-stick cooking spray.

○ Rinse steak and pat dry.

○ Place steak in a medium bowl. Pour teriyaki sauce over it, turning steak to coat all sides. Set aside.

○ In a medium skillet, heat oil over medium-high heat. Add onions and mushrooms, and sauté for 8 to 10 minutes or until softened.

○ Spread vegetables over bottom of prepared roasting pan. Place steak on top.

○ Bake at 450° for 40 minutes for medium, or to desired doneness.

○ Let stand at room temperature for 5 minutes. Slice against the grain into 1-inch thick slices. Serve with vegetables over hot rice, if desired.

To cut down on those dirty dishes, start with a pan that can go from the stove top straight to the broiler.

PREP: 5 minutes
COOK: 2 hours, 15 minutes
CHILL: none
YIELD: 8 to 10 servings

Mushroom and Wine Silver Tip Roast

1   (4-pound) silver tip beef roast
1   large onion, sliced
½   teaspoon paprika
½   teaspoon kosher salt
½   teaspoon black pepper
½   teaspoon garlic powder
½   cup dry red wine
1   (8-ounce) carton sliced mushrooms

○ Preheat oven to 350° F. Lightly grease a roasting pan with non-stick cooking spray.

○ Rinse roast, pat dry and place in prepared pan. Surround with onions.

○ Rub paprika, salt, pepper and garlic powder into roast.

○ Pour wine over roast and onions (add a little oil if it is lean).

○ Bake, covered, at 350° for 1 hour. Remove pan from oven and place mushrooms around the roast. Cover, return to oven and bake for 1 more hour, or to desired doneness.

○ Let stand 5 to 10 minutes at room temperature before slicing diagonally against the grain.

○ Arrange on platter with vegetables on top. Pass pan juices in a sauce boat.

Suggested Wine: Hagafen 2002 Estate Bottled Napa Valley Cabernet Sauvignon. Roast calls for a wine that will complement – not overwhelm – its meatiness. This delicate Cab, with its higher acids and licorice spice, will do that well. For added matching, use the wine in the recipe.

157

Beef Sukiyaki with Noodles

1 cup soy sauce
½ cup white wine
½ cup seasoned rice vinegar
4 tablespoons sugar
2 pounds pepper steak strips
3 tablespoons olive oil, divided
2 medium onions, sliced
5 scallions, sliced
1 (6-ounce) package sliced portobello mushrooms
1 (7-ounce) package baby spinach leaves
1 (16-ounce) box fettuccini, cooked according to package directions

PREP: 9 minutes
COOK: 15 minutes
CHILL: none
YIELD: 8 servings

159

○ Mix soy sauce, wine, vinegar and sugar in a small bowl until sugar dissolves; set aside.

○ Rinse pepper steak and pat dry.

○ Heat 2 tablespoons oil in a large, deep skillet over medium heat. Add pepper steak and sauté for 2 to 4 minutes, until almost cooked through. Remove from skillet and set aside.

○ Add remaining oil to skillet and sauté onions, scallions and mushrooms for 5 minutes.

○ Add spinach and cook for 1 minute, until wilted.

○ Return pepper steak to skillet with vegetables and add ¾ of the soy sauce mixture. Bring to boil. Reduce heat and simmer, uncovered, for 1 minute.

○ Place meat and vegetable mixture in a large warm serving bowl. Add fettuccini and toss. Drizzle with remaining soy mixture before serving.

Suggested Wine: Hagafen 2005 Potter Valley White Riesling.
Perhaps an idiosyncratic choice, Riesling works because its high acid will contrast against the soy and sugar, whereas most red wines will falter in the face of those flavors.

The word *yaki* means "sauté" or "grill" in Japanese. The best beef for sukiyaki is a cut that has lots of fat but is still very tender. For a splurge, ask your butcher to slice top chuck French roast into pepper steak-like strips.

This recipe is adapted from *Food & Wine* magazine. It called for sake, a traditional Japanese wine fermented from rice, I substituted white wine, as it is hard to find kosher sake.

London Broil

1   (2-3 pound) London broil, thin-cut
½   cup barbecue sauce
¼   cup ketchup
1   tablespoon garlic salt
1   tablespoon onion powder

○ Preheat broiler. Lightly grease a broiler pan with non-stick cooking spray.

○ Rinse beef and pat dry.

○ Place beef and all other ingredients in a large sealable plastic bag. Place in refrigerator and marinate for 15 minutes. Turn bag over and marinate for another 15 minutes.

○ Place beef in prepared pan. Discard excess marinade.

○ Broil at high heat in preheated broiler for approximately 5 minutes.

○ Turn beef over and continue broiling for approximately 4 to 5 minutes for medium rare or to desired doneness.

○ Remove meat from broiler pan to another surface to rest. Let beef stand 5 to 10 minutes before slicing diagonally against the grain.

This recipe is just heavenly served over mashed potatoes!

Suggested Wine: Hagafen 2004 Reserve Estate Bottled Napa Valley Pinot Noir Fagan Creek Vineyard: Block 38. Broiled meat in combination with barbecue sauce requires a wine with depth and smokiness. This Pinot Noir is a perfect match in both aroma and taste.

Asian Steak

PREP: 5 minutes

COOK: 2 hours, 35 minutes

CHILL: none

YIELD: 4 servings

4   tablespoons olive oil

2   pounds chuck steak, bone-in, 1-inch thick

2   tablespoons light brown sugar

3   tablespoons soy sauce

1   large onion, sliced

2   cups boiling water

2   tablespoons Osem Consommé Mix

1   large celery stalk, sliced

1   (8-ounce) can sliced water chestnuts, drained

1/8   teaspoon coarse black pepper

     Pimientos, diced, for garnish

○ Heat olive oil in a large, deep skillet over medium-high heat.

○ Rinse steak and pat dry. Place in skillet and brown on both sides, about 1 to 2 minutes per side. Drain off oil.

○ Add brown sugar, soy sauce, onion, water, consommé mix, celery, water chestnuts, and pepper. Make sure steak and vegetables are submerged in liquid mixture.

○ Reduce heat and simmer, covered, for 2 hours and 30 minutes or until steak is tender.

○ Garnish with pimientos before serving.

Another winner from Grandma Martha Geller's treasure chest inspired by a New York Times recipe published a few decades back. She told me to put everything in the pan in stages – but of course, I didn't listen.

I wish all chefs would try making their recipes easy first. It seems to me they make them complicated and time-consuming on purpose: "In 1 hour add celery; twiddle your thumbs and wash your hair; and an hour later, add the water chestnuts." Do you find that everyone seems to be working backwards, from more complicated to simpler, or is it just me?

Suggested Wine: Hagafen 2001 Estate Bottled Napa Valley Syrah. You'll want a wine that can cut through the soy, brown sugar and celery of this sauce. The 2001 Syrah will do just that thanks to its leather and tobacco notes.

Lamb Chops with Pistachio Crust

1 cup salted pistachios, shelled

$\frac{1}{3}$ teaspoon kosher salt

$\frac{1}{4}$ teaspoon coarse black pepper

2 tablespoons olive oil

4 (1-inch thick) shoulder lamb chops

○ Preheat broiler. Lightly grease a broiler pan with non-stick cooking spray.

○ Crush pistachios in food processor until finely chopped, about 30 seconds; you should have about $\frac{1}{2}$ cup.

○ Mix ground nuts, salt and pepper and place on a plate.

○ Pour olive oil onto another plate.

○ Rinse lamb chops and pat dry.

○ Dip chops in olive oil and then in pistachio mixture to coat all surfaces.

○ Place chops in prepared broiler pan.

○ Broil lamb chops for 7 minutes on each side for medium to medium rare, or longer depending on desired degree of doneness. Serve immediately.

My hubby worked in catering for a long time, and he reminisces nostalgically about the pistachio-crusted baby lamb chops they used to serve. Baby lamb chops are tender and delicious, but to make enough for 4 people would take more than 15 minutes. However, if you have the time, roll up your sleeves and use the baby chops. You'll need about 3 to 4 per person.

Suggested Wine: Hagafen 2002 Estate Bottled Napa Valley Cabernet Sauvignon. **Many Cabs would be too heavy to let the flavors of the lamb shine through, but this Cab, crafted as a food wine, with its high acid and licorice and cranberry essence will nicely complement the pistachio crust.**

Beef Goulash

3 tablespoons canola oil or olive oil

2 pounds cubed stew beef

2 large onions, sliced

2 cloves garlic, peeled, minced

1 cup ketchup

2 tablespoons Worcestershire sauce
 (see note, p. 139)

1 tablespoon brown sugar, packed

1 tablespoon paprika

1 teaspoon yellow mustard

2 teaspoons salt

1¼ cups water, divided

2 tablespoons flour

 Wide egg noodles cooked according
 to package directions (optional)

PREP: 8 minutes

COOK: 2 hours, 15 minutes

CHILL: none

YIELD: 6 servings

○ Heat oil in 3- or 4-quart pot over high heat.

○ Rinse beef, pat dry and place in pot. Brown the meat on all sides, about 10 minutes.

○ Add onions and garlic and sauté for 2 to 3 minutes.

○ Add ketchup, Worcestershire sauce, sugar, paprika, mustard, salt and ¾ cup water. Mix well.

○ Simmer, covered, for 1 hour and 30 minutes, checking and adding a little more water if needed. Continue to simmer uncovered for remaining 30 minutes.

○ Right before serving, blend flour and remaining water to make a smooth paste. Gradually stir into meat mixture.

○ Heat to boiling and stir for 1 minute to thicken. Serve hot, over cooked wide egg noodles, if desired.

Suggested Wine: Hagafen 2001 Estate Bottled Napa Valley Syrah.
Spicy goulash needs a wine with high acid and its own spice to cut through the sauce. This Syrah will do so ably; its leather and solid tannins will up the impact of the dish.

○ Also known as *gulyás*, this dish was invented by Hungarian cowboys, who stewed and sun-dried cubed beef over a campfire. *Gulyá* means "herd of cattle" or "cowboy" and *hús* means "meat." Put the words together and you have meat, cowboy-style.

164

PREP: 8 minutes

COOK: overnight

CHILL: none

YIELD: 8 servings

Family Heirloom Chulent

2   medium potatoes, peeled and cut
     into bite-sized chunks

2   medium onions, cut into bite-sized
     chunks

1   (2-pound) piece of flanken,
     cut into 4 to 6 pieces

1/2 tablespoon coarse black pepper

3/4 cup barley

1   cup dried light red kidney beans

3   tablespoons Osem Consommé Mix

2   tablespoons paprika

2   tablespoons honey

1   (1-pound) kishka loaf

3   cups water

○ Line bottom of slow cooker with potatoes
  and onions.

○ Rinse flanken and pat dry. Place pieces
  around sides of crock pot, with bones
  on the outside.

○ Generously pepper the meat.

○ Add barley and beans. Shake the pot a
  bit so some of the barley and beans fall
  into the spaces between the potatoes
  and onions.

○ Season with consommé mix, paprika and
  honey.

○ Place kishka on top.

○ Pour in water, adding more if necessary,
  to completely cover all ingredients.

○ Cook on low heat overnight, at least
  8 hours.

This recipe used to be top secret. My husband made it for Shabbos every week
and he never divulged the details, even
to me! Then one Friday he wasn't feeling well and rather than give up his
weekly chulent, he let me take over. I
was so nervous.

It wasn't a success the first time, but
I've practiced and now we're neck and
neck. It was his father's recipe, passed
on to his older brother, then passed on
to him. It was supposed to go straight
to our son (whom, G-d willing, we will
have one day) but I got it first! I guess
you could say I am now an honorary
member of the men's club.

The Yiddish word for chulent comes
from the French word for warm, *chaud*.
Sephardic Jews call this dish *chamin*,
which means the same thing.

Lamb Chops on a Bed of Couscous

1   teaspoon dried sage or
      1 tablespoon fresh sage, minced

1   teaspoon kosher salt

½   teaspoon coarse black pepper

2   tablespoons olive oil

6-8   shoulder lamb chops, about
      2½ pounds

¼   cup white wine

1   tablespoon red wine vinegar

6-8   mint leaves, chopped

1   (5.6 ounce) box Near East Toasted
      Pine Nut Couscous, prepared
      according to package directions

○ In a small bowl, mix sage, salt and pepper.

○ Rinse lamb chops and pat dry. Rub spice
  mixture into chops.

○ Heat oil in a large skillet over medium heat.

○ Place lamb chops in skillet. Fry for 6 to
  7 minutes on each side for medium rare.

○ Drain off excess fat. Add wine, vinegar
  and mint.

○ Cover and cook for 1 to 2 minutes. Remove
  from heat.

○ Spoon couscous onto a serving platter.
  Arrange lamb chops on top and serve.

Suggested Wine: Hagafen 2000 Estate Bottled Napa Valley Syrah.
Gamey, meaty lamb will pair well with the licorice and cloves of the
2000 Syrah. The mint leaves, too, will find their complement in this wine.

Veal Stew with Apricots and Prunes

PREP: 9 minutes
COOK: 1 hour, 10 minutes
CHILL: none
YIELD: 6 to 8 servings

4	tablespoons olive oil
2	onions, coarsely chopped or cut into wedges
¼	cup tomato paste
2-3	pounds veal stew meat, cut into 1-inch cubes
1	teaspoon salt
½	teaspoon coarse black pepper
16	baby carrots, halved, length-wise
3	cups water
¾	cup dried apricots
¾	cup dried prunes

○ Heat oil in 4-quart pot over medium heat.

○ Place onions in pot and sauté for 8 to 10 minutes or until just beginning to brown. Add tomato paste and stir continuously for 2 to 3 minutes.

○ Rinse veal and pat dry; season with salt and pepper.

○ Add veal to pot and brown for approximately 10 minutes.

○ Add carrots and water.

○ Bring to a boil. Reduce heat and simmer, covered, for 40 minutes.

○ Add apricots and prunes and continue to simmer, uncovered, for 5 minutes or until veal is soft and sauce thickens.

Suggested Wine: Hagafen 2003 Estate Bottled Napa Valley Merlot. The twist here is the softness of the veal in contrast to the sweetness of the carrots, apricots and prunes. The licorice and bergamot in this Merlot will accent those flavors.

PREP: 6 minutes
COOK: 8 to 10 hours
CHILL: none
YIELD: 8 to 10 servings

Slow Cooked Lamb Stew

3-4 pounds lamb stew, cubed

2   medium potatoes, peeled and cut into chunks

3   cloves garlic

1   (22-ounce) can diced tomatoes, drained

1   (10-ounce) bag frozen chopped onions

1   (16-ounce) bag frozen sliced carrots

1   cup barley

1   teaspoon kosher salt

1   cup beef broth or 1 cup boiling water mixed with 1 tablespoon Osem Beef Soup Mix

1   tablespoon dried parsley flakes

1   teaspoon dried, crumbled thyme

$^1/_3$ cup dry red wine

$^1/_2$ cup prepared marinara sauce

- Lightly grease slow cooker with non-stick cooking spray.

- Rinse lamb and pat dry. Place all ingredients in slow cooker and stir to mix.

- Cover and cook 8 to 10 hours on low, or as an option, 4 to 5 hours on high.

- Ladle into bowls and serve immediately.

Suggested Wine: Hagafen 2002 Estate Bottled Napa Valley Syrah. Slow-cooked lamb loses a bit of its gaminess while gaining a depth of flavor. That requires the cloves and spices of this Syrah to perk up the mouthfeel.

I asked my friend Monet for the recipe for this dish three years after I had it at her house. She could only remember the ingredients, so we improvised – with happy results.

Barbecued Meatloaf

PREP: 5 minutes
COOK: 1 hour
CHILL: none
YIELD: 6 to 8 servings

2   pounds ground beef

1   egg

³/₄   cup bread crumbs

¹/₂   cup barbecue sauce

2   tablespoons onion powder

2   tablespoons garlic powder

1   tablespoon dried parsley flakes

○ Preheat oven to 350° F. Lightly grease a 9 x 5 x 3-inch loaf pan with non-stick cooking spray.

○ Place all ingredients in a large bowl. Mix well.

○ Press into prepared loaf pan.

○ Bake, uncovered, at 350° for 1 hour.

○ Loosen edges of meatloaf with a blunt-edged knife and turn meatloaf out onto a platter. Slice and serve.

I made my first meatloaf when I had a ton of leftover ground beef from trying my hand at meatballs. We were having a few guests for Shabbos, and as I was filling the pot with enough meatballs to feed an army, Hubby suggested I use the remaining meatball mixture for meatloaf. "I can't serve that at a Shabbos meal!" I said. "It's so unattractive and ordinary." Hubby assured me it would be wonderful.

At dinnertime, I brought it to the table, apologizing every step of the way. And surprise, it was such a huge hit! More people complimented the meatloaf than the meatballs. It has since evolved into this unique barbecued version.

○ Place a few hard-cooked eggs in the middle of the loaf before baking. Or make a shepherd's pie by adding either instant or homemade mashed potatoes. Spread a layer of potatoes over the beef before baking.

Grandma's Meatballs

PREP: 10 minutes
COOK: 1 hour, 20 minutes
CHILL: none
YIELD: 8 servings

1   egg
2   pounds ground beef
3   (26-ounce) jars prepared marinara
     sauce, divided
¼   cup seltzer
¼   cup dried minced onion flakes
2   tablespoons seasoned bread crumbs
1   tablespoon garlic powder
⅛   teaspoon coarse black pepper

○ In a large bowl, beat egg for about 30 seconds.

○ Add ground beef, 2 tablespoons marinara sauce, seltzer, onion flakes, bread crumbs, garlic powder and pepper. Using clean hands, mix well but lightly.

○ Pour remaining marinara from first jar into a 6-quart pot.

○ Shape meat mixture into 16 medium-sized meatballs. As you are shaping meatballs, place them in the pot with the marinara sauce; make sure meatballs do not touch sides of pot.

○ When you have a layer of meatballs, add another jar of sauce, and begin the next layer of meatballs.

○ Cover with the remaining jar of sauce. Bring to a boil, and then reduce heat and simmer, covered, for 1 hour and 20 minutes. Occasionally stir the meatballs very carefully, so they don't fall apart and don't burn on the bottom layer.

This recipe was given to me by my hubby's Grandma Martha. It's been in her recipe box so long that no one knows its exact origins. All we know is that it's a surefire success. It gives you a light, fluffy meatball every time.

Meatballs are a real crowd pleaser with children. They are also a great complement to Challah Kugel (page 189), or Potato Kugel Cups (page 191), as both go well with a gravy or marinara sauce. For dinner during the week, just boil up a pot of spaghetti, toss on the meatballs and you're done.

Shish Kebab

175

2   pounds beef chuck, cut into 1-inch pieces

1   cup teriyaki sauce

12   medium white mushrooms

12   medium grape tomatoes

○ Rinse beef, pat dry and place in a bowl.

○ Add teriyaki sauce and stir to coat all surfaces of the beef. Place in refrigerator and marinate for at least 1 hour.

○ Before preparing skewers, preheat broiler. Lightly grease a large broiler pan with non-stick cooking spray.

○ To assemble skewers: Remove beef from marinade. Spear beef and vegetables on each skewer as follows: 1 piece marinated beef, 1 mushroom, 1 piece marinated beef, 1 tomato, ending with marinated beef.

○ Place on prepared broiler pan.

○ Broil 5 minutes on each side.

○ If using wooden skewers as opposed to metal ones, soak them in water while you are prepping. This step will prevent the wood from burning.

Side dishes are usually relegated to the back of a cookbook. They seem to be an afterthought, the extras nobody needs, while the main course gets all the attention and glory. But when I was a vegetarian, I used to live on sides. They were my main course, usually my whole meal. A veggie's habits die hard. So you can trust that all the sides in this section were given the love, care and attention to detail that any fine beef brisket or rib roast would receive. The sides in *my* book are stars, too.

Sides
That (Really) Are a Cinch

Kugel is a classic side dish in many Jewish homes. But most kugel recipes take roughly the same amount of time as putting together a 10-speed bike. It was my sister-in-law Abbie who first told me that it was okay to just throw everything in a bowl. She saved me from impending mother-in-law / daughter-in-law disaster. Here's the story:

My husband's stepmother, Judy, once gave me a recipe for broccoli kugel, making a big deal out of how it was perfect for me because it's so easy. (Thanks, Judy.) She began her directions: First I was to separate the eggs. Confused right off the bat, I thought "separate the eggs?" Did that mean two eggs to the left, two eggs to the right?

When she saw my puzzled look, she explained it meant separating the yolks from the whites. Then I was supposed to beat the whites until they were stiff, forming soft peaks. In my opinion, this was no easy as pie, 1-2-3 recipe. I don't have time to separate my laundry, whites from colors, and she wants me to separate eggs?

As if that weren't enough, she then told me to take frozen broccoli cuts and throw them in the blender to chop them even finer, into itsy-bitsy, teeny-weeny broccoli specks. It seemed like no one could understand what I meant by "really fast and easy" recipes!

I was utterly distressed. There was no way I could produce a broccoli kugel that would impress Judy. When I spoke to Abbie, she said that she had an easy, 1-2-3 recipe for broccoli kugel that would save the day and my pride. I didn't believe her at first. She'd probably start by telling me to separate the eggs.

No, she said, the eggs in her recipe require no separating and no beating, no coaxing and no peaks. Just dump them with some mayo and frozen broccoli cuts – straight from the bag! – into a baking dish. I felt like the gates of heaven had opened and angels were singing. Someone finally had the same definition I did of "fast," "easy" and "1-2-3." If we hadn't been on the phone, I would have picked her up and kissed her.

So I tried it. And dear Abbie gets the prize. This kugel's so delicious that every time I serve it, Judy asks where I got the recipe. I think the magic is in using the broccoli cuts as is. Biting into a nice broccoli floret here and there makes it feel like a real, hearty vegetable side, as opposed to a puréed, albeit delicious, green square.

Yes, Abbie's recipe is in this chapter, along with plenty of other "fast and easy, 1-2-3" sides. You know what I mean.

PREP: 4 minutes
COOK: 5 minutes
CHILL: none
YIELD: 4 servings

Broiled Tomatoes

2 large beefsteak tomatoes, halved (horizontally)

8 tablespoons flavored bread crumbs

1 frozen crushed garlic cube

3 tablespoons olive oil

¼ teaspoon salt

¼ teaspoon pepper

- Turn on broiler. Lightly grease a broiler pan with non-stick cooking spray.

- Using a spoon, remove seeds from tomatoes and place tomato halves in prepared pan.

- In a small bowl, mix bread crumbs, garlic, olive oil, salt and pepper.

- Sprinkle bread crumb mixture evenly on each tomato.

- Broil for 5 minutes and serve immediately.

I love fresh tomatoes. Even as a kid in summer camp, I made a friend on the kitchen staff so I could have tomatoes smuggled to me. My taste buds haven't changed, just evolved. Nowadays, I love grape tomatoes, plum tomatoes or the expensive, imported Israeli or Holland tomatoes on the vine. Every now and then they're worth the splurge.

If you're having a dairy meal, sprinkle a little parmesan or shredded mozzarella cheese on each tomato before broiling.

PREP: 6 minutes
COOK: 15 minutes
CHILL: none
YIELD: 4 servings

Italian Zucchini

2   tablespoons olive oil

1   onion, coarsely chopped

2   zucchini, thinly sliced

2   teaspoons prepared crushed garlic

½   teaspoon crumbled, dried oregano

½   teaspoon salt

½   teaspoon pepper

○ Heat oil in a large skillet over medium heat.

○ Add onion and sauté 2 minutes.

○ Add zucchini, garlic, oregano, salt and pepper, and sauté for 3 minutes.

○ Reduce heat to low, cover and cook for 10 minutes. Serve immediately.

For more flavor and pizzazz, add and sauté a carton of fresh sliced mushroom and some red bell pepper strips. Season with a little extra garlic, oregano, salt and pepper to taste.

Baked Spicy
Sweet Potato Fries

PREP: 15 minutes

COOK: 1 hour

CHILL: none

YIELD: 4 servings

3   large sweet potatoes, cut into $\frac{1}{3}$-inch thick sticks

$\frac{3}{4}$ teaspoon ground cumin

1   teaspoon garlic powder

2   teaspoons kosher salt

$\frac{1}{8}$ teaspoon cayenne pepper

1   teaspoon coarse black pepper

$\frac{1}{4}$ cup canola oil

   Ketchup or honey mustard (optional)

○ Preheat oven to 425° F. Lightly grease two 9 x 13-inch baking pans with non-stick cooking spray.

○ Place cut potatoes in prepared pans.

○ In a small bowl, mix cumin, garlic powder, salt and peppers, and sprinkle over potatoes.

○ Drizzle oil over potatoes. Toss to distribute olive oil and seasonings evenly.

○ Bake at 425° for 1 hour or until crunchy on the outside and tender on the inside.

○ Serve with ketchup or honey mustard on the side, if desired.

181

Again, my thanks to my good friend Monet, not just for introducing me to these spices in general, but also for this delicious recipe that any fry lover (I tested it out on the Fry King – my hubby!) will adore.

Baby French String Beans with Slivered Almonds

PREP: 10 minutes

COOK: 15 minutes

CHILL: none

YIELD: 6 servings

1   pound baby French string beans

1   cup water

1   tablespoon soy sauce

¼   cup toasted sesame oil

½   cup slivered almonds

2   tablespoons prepared crushed garlic

1   tablespoon sesame seeds

1   teaspoon sea salt

○ Wash and trim stem end of beans. Do not trim the thin, elegant end. Place in a medium saucepan.

○ Stir in remaining ingredients.

○ Cover partially, allowing a bit of air to escape. Bring to a simmer over low heat and cook for 15 minutes or until tender.

○ Pour into a bowl and serve warm or cold.

Haricots verts is the official French name for these delicious, best-ever green beans. They are slender, more flavorful, stringless string beans. You can easily use regular string beans for this recipe, if you prefer. Just cook them about 5 minutes longer.

Savory Eggplant

1   cup olive oil

½   cup balsamic vinegar

1   medium eggplant, stem end removed,
     cut into ½-inch thick slices

½   teaspoon garlic powder or
     1 teaspoon prepared crushed garlic

¼   teaspoon crumbled, dried oregano

½   teaspoon paprika

½   teaspoon salt

○ Preheat oven to 450° F. Lightly spray a
  cookie sheet with non-stick cooking spray.

○ Place olive oil and vinegar in a bowl and
  whisk together. Add eggplant slices,
  tossing to coat.

○ Place eggplant in one layer on prepared
  cookie sheet.

○ Sprinkle evenly with garlic, oregano, paprika
  and salt.

○ Bake, uncovered, at 450° for 10 to 12 minutes
  or until softened.

○ Serve hot or at room temperature.

If you have extra time, broil on one
side for 4 minutes and turn over to
broil the other side for 3 minutes
to evenly brown.

Cranberry Relish

PREP: 4 minutes
COOK: none
CHILL: 1 hour
YIELD: 6 servings

1   (16-ounce) can whole berry
    cranberry sauce
1   (20-ounce) can crushed or chunk
    pineapple, drained
$1/4$ cup chopped walnuts
$1/2$ teaspoon cinnamon
$1/4$ teaspoon nutmeg

○ Place cranberry sauce in a medium bowl.

○ Mix in pineapple, walnuts, cinnamon and nutmeg.

○ Chill in refrigerator for 1 hour before serving.

185

Though it's a luscious complement for turkey, you'll find yourself eating this relish all by itself. I usually have trouble getting it to the table without digging in first. Make an extra batch to lure your family into finishing the turkey leftovers.

PREP: 4 minutes

COOK: 10 minutes

CHILL: none

YIELD: 4 servings

Curried Coconut Couscous

1	tablespoon olive oil
1½	teaspoons curry powder
4	dried apricots, cut into thin strips
½	cup canned coconut milk
¾	cup water
¾	cup Near East Original Plain Couscous
1	cup unsweetened coconut flakes
1	teaspoon cinnamon
1	tablespoon orange juice
½	tablespoon honey
¼	teaspoon salt
	Fresh mint leaves (optional)

○ Heat olive oil in a 3-quart saucepan. Add curry powder and cook for a minute to release flavor.

○ Add apricots, coconut milk and water, and bring to a boil.

○ Stir in couscous, coconut flakes, cinnamon, orange juice, honey and salt. Combine thoroughly but quickly.

○ Remove from heat and let stand, covered, for 5 minutes. Fluff with a fork and serve warm or cold, garnished with a few fresh mint leaves if desired.

Couscous, which is a small round pasta made of semolina grain and water, is originally of North African or Berber origins. It is popular in parts of the Middle East, Algeria, eastern Morocco, Tunisia and Libya, where it is so basic that it is known as *ta`aam*, meaning "food." It is often served with meat or vegetable stews.

Broccoli Kugel

PREP: 5 minutes
COOK: 1 hour, 15 minutes
CHILL: none
YIELD: 8 servings

1   (2-pound) bag frozen chopped broccoli cuts, thawed and drained

1   cup light mayonnaise

4   eggs

½   tablespoon kosher salt

¼   teaspoon coarse black pepper

1   pinch cayenne pepper

○ Preheat oven to 375° F.

○ Liberally grease a 9-inch round baking dish with non-stick cooking spray.

○ In a large bowl place broccoli, mayonnaise, eggs, salt, black and cayenne peppers and mix well.

○ Pour broccoli mixture into prepared baking dish.

○ Bake at 375° for 1 hour and 15 minutes until set and edges are golden brown.

The recipe I promised you! This easy and tasty side was one of the inspirations for this book, and with good reason.

The word *kugel* is German for "ball" and probably refers to the small round pot in which kugels used to be cooked. The pot would be placed inside the chulent pot and left there to cook until served on Shabbos. Eventually kugels were baked separately in larger pans.

Challah Kugel

PREP: 15 minutes

COOK: 45 minutes

CHILL: none

YIELD: 6 to 8 servings

2   tablespoons olive oil

2   large loaves day-old or stale water challah, crusts removed and cubed as for croutons

2   tablespoons Osem Consommé Mix

⅛   teaspoon coarse black pepper

3   eggs, beaten

1   teaspoon baking powder

2   tablespoons seasoned bread crumbs

○ Preheat oven to 400° F.

○ Place oil in a 9 x 5 x 3-inch loaf pan and place in oven.

○ Place cubed challah in a colander and wet it quickly and lightly; put your fingers under the running water to lighten the flow, moving the colander so none of the bread gets too wet. Sprinkle with just enough water to dampen challah; do not drench it. Squeeze out excess water. Challah should look and feel like wet rags.

○ In a large bowl, gently fold together challah, consommé mix, pepper, eggs, baking powder and bread crumbs. Don't over mix, but evenly disperse ingredients. The mixture should still be lumpy.

○ Remove loaf pan from oven and pour challah mixture into loaf pan.

○ Lower oven temperature to 375°. Bake, uncovered, for 45 minutes until top is golden to dark brown and crunchy.

○ Cut into squares and serve warm. If not serving immediately, cool upside down on a clean dish towel. Refrigerate and re-heat before serving.

189

My very first real success! Thanks to Grandma Martha's patience, I have now mastered her famous recipe – most probably because I made her stay on the phone and walk me through each step "holding my hand" and offering much needed emotional support.

I bake this kugel in our family-heirloom, grease-stained, metal loaf pan. To my surprise, it even comes out great (with the quantities doubled) in a 9 x 13-inch disposable pan! It's a dish made from leftovers, yet a novelty at the table. What could be better?

Water challah is essential to this dish's success: Do not use egg challah.

If you don't have enough leftover scraps, you can fake stale old bread. Just bake slices of fresh bread on a cookie sheet for approximately 30 minutes at about 200° F.

Potato Kugel Cups

PREP: 15 minutes

COOK: 1 hour

CHILL: none

YIELD: 4 to 6 servings

3/4   cup olive oil, divided

3   eggs

2   teaspoons kosher salt

1/2   teaspoon coarse black pepper

6   large Idaho potatoes

1   large onion, quartered

- Preheat oven to 425° F.

- Liberally oil six (6-ounce) Pyrex glass dessert dishes or custard cups. Place custard cups in a 9 x 13-inch disposable pan.

- Place the pan of cups in the oven to heat.

- Place eggs in a small bowl and beat. Add salt and pepper, mix well and set aside.

- Fill a large bowl with cold water and as you peel potatoes, place them in water to prevent browning.

- Heat remainder of oil in a small saucepan on the stove over medium-low heat.

- Cut potatoes lengthwise into halves or quarters so they fit into food processor feed tube. Process potatoes and onions using the blade that creates thin, shoe-string-like strips.

- Transfer potatoes and onions to a large bowl, add egg mixture and heated oil from stovetop, mix very well. Remove any large pieces of potatoes or onions that weren't processed properly.

- Remove heated cups from the oven and spoon potato mixture evenly into hot, oiled cups.

- Bake at 425° for 1 hour, or until the tops look crunchy and sides look golden and browned. Loosen edges with a knife, un-mold and serve on a platter.

191

This famous potato kugel, the one I mentioned in "Setting Up Your Kitchen," is based on my friend Lauren's recipe, though she swears by using red-skinned potatoes. The cup idea comes from my husband's best friend Adam's mom, Geanie (what a mouthful). Hubby remembers going to their house on Saturday nights and raiding the fridge for these cups. The best part about them is that every piece is a crusty corner piece, so nobody has to fight over that coveted crunch.

Make this in a 9-inch round glass baking dish as a potato kugel pie and bake for about 1 hour or longer, depending on desired crunchiness.

Latkes
(Potato Pancakes)

PREP: 12 minutes

COOK: 18 to 24 minutes

CHILL: none

YIELD: 8 servings

4   medium Idaho potatoes

6   tablespoons canola oil or olive oil

3   eggs, beaten

2   tablespoons matzoh meal

2   teaspoons kosher salt

$\frac{1}{2}$ teaspoon coarse black pepper

    Applesauce or sour cream (optional)

○ Prepare a large bowl filled with cold water.

○ Peel potatoes, and as you finish each, place in cold water to prevent browning.

○ Heat oil in a large skillet over medium heat.

○ Cut potatoes lengthwise into halves or quarters so they fit into food processor feed tube. Process potatoes using the blade that creates thin, shoestring-like strips and transfer to a large bowl.

○ Add eggs, matzoh meal, salt and pepper and mix well.

○ Drop 6 to 8 spoonfuls of mixture into hot oil. Using the back of a spoon, pat down each latke to flatten it. Put as many as you can in the skillet without crowding. Putting them too close together will make them soggy.

○ Fry 3 to 4 minutes on each side, until golden and crisp around the edges; repeat procedure until finished with all the batter.

○ Blot excess oil with paper towels.

○ Serve warm with applesauce or sour cream, if desired.

Just like they used to do it in the old country! These latkes are not loaded with potato starch, flour, baking powder or other non-essential ingredients. My grandfather shared this recipe with me when I told him that I thought his were the crunchiest, lightest and most perfect potato latkes I've ever eaten.

Corn meal is a great substitute for matzoh meal and will also make your latkes nice and crispy.

Broccoli and Mushroom Pie

PREP: 6 minutes

COOK: 1 hour to
1 hour, 15 minutes

CHILL: none

YIELD: 8 servings

1   (10-ounce) box frozen chopped broccoli cuts, thawed and drained

1   (8-ounce) carton sliced mushrooms

1   (9-inch) frozen deep dish prepared piecrust

1   medium onion, diced

4   eggs, lightly beaten

1   cup liquid non-dairy creamer

2   tablespoons flour

1   teaspoon salt

1/2   teaspoon black pepper

○ Preheat oven to 375° F.

○ Arrange broccoli and mushrooms in piecrust.

○ In a bowl, place onion, eggs, non-dairy creamer, flour, salt and pepper. Mix to combine. Pour over vegetables.

○ Bake at 375° for 1 hour to 1 hour and 15 minutes, until mixture is set.

○ Use a pie server to cut into wedge-shaped pieces; serve warm.

Loosely cover with aluminum foil if center is not yet set but crust is browning too fast.

Broccolini in a Creamy Wine Balsamic Sauce

PREP: 7 minutes
COOK: 4 to 6 minutes
CHILL: none
YIELD: 6 servings

5   cups water

3   pounds broccolini

For Sauce:

2   tablespoons balsamic vinegar

½   tablespoon red wine

2   tablespoons liquid non-dairy creamer

2   tablespoons olive oil

1   tablespoon Dijon-style mustard

1   tablespoon light brown sugar

1   tablespoon garlic powder

○ In a medium saucepan, bring water to a boil over high heat.

○ Add broccolini and boil for 4 to 6 minutes, or until bright green and barely tender. Drain well. Transfer to a serving dish and keep warm.

○ Combine all sauce ingredients in saucepan and heat through, stirring continuously. Remove from heat and beat until smooth and creamy.

○ Drizzle sauce over broccolini, serving any additional sauce on the side.

195

This creamy wine balsamic sauce is good over any greens of your choice. If you like plain ol' broccoli, endive, collard greens or even kale, use them. My hubby says I'm the only one who eats kale by itself and that most caterers just use it for a garnish or to decorate a platter. Show him he's wrong! He always needs to be right, you know. The problem is that I do, too!

Broccolini is a cross between broccoli and Chinese kale.

Garlicky Broccoli

3   tablespoons olive oil

2   cloves garlic, peeled, chopped

$\frac{1}{2}$ teaspoon rosemary

2   (1-pound) bags frozen broccoli spears, thawed and drained

1   teaspoon kosher salt

$\frac{1}{2}$ teaspoon coarse black pepper

○ In a large skillet, heat olive oil and sauté garlic and rosemary over medium heat for 1 minute.

○ Add broccoli. Sprinkle with salt and pepper.

○ Continue to sauté for 5 minutes longer, stirring constantly. Broccoli should be bright green and barely tender. Serve immediately.

Herb-Roasted
Red Bliss Potatoes

3   pounds baby red bliss potatoes,
    halved

½   cup olive oil

2   tablespoons dried parsley flakes or
    4 tablespoons fresh minced parsley

2   tablespoons onion powder

1   tablespoon garlic powder or 2 table-
    spoons prepared crushed garlic

1½ teaspoons crumbled, dried oregano

1½ teaspoons kosher salt

1   teaspoon coarse black pepper

○ Preheat oven to 400° F. Spray two 9 x 13-
   inch pans with non-stick cooking spray.

○ Divide potatoes evenly between the two
   prepared pans and drizzle with olive oil.
   Toss to coat.

○ In a small bowl, mix parsley, onion and
   garlic powders, oregano, salt and pepper. Sprinkle over potatoes and toss to
   distribute evenly.

○ Roast, uncovered, at 400° for 30 to 40
   minutes or until potatoes are soft inside
   and crisp and golden brown outside.

○ Serve hot.

You may have already noticed by now
that I love all things mini. In potatoes,
that means baby red bliss, fingerlings
and the small white variety sometimes
sold as "creamers." Use any combination of mini potatoes for this recipe.

Roasted Sweet Vegetables in Spicy Cinnamon Cider

PREP: 12 minutes

COOK: 1 hour, 30 minutes

CHILL: none

YIELD: 6 to 8 servings

1   cup sweet apple cider

2   tablespoons white wine vinegar

2   tablespoons margarine

2   tablespoons olive oil

1   tablespoon lemon juice

$\frac{1}{2}$ cup brown sugar, packed

$4\frac{1}{2}$ teaspoons cinnamon

$\frac{1}{2}$ teaspoon nutmeg

1   tablespoon kosher salt

$\frac{1}{4}$ teaspoon cayenne pepper or to taste

2   large sweet potatoes, peeled and cut into chunks

1   pound prepared peeled, cubed butternut squash

25   baby carrots

$\frac{1}{2}$ cup raisins

$\frac{1}{2}$ cup golden raisins

○ Preheat oven to 375° F. Lightly grease a roasting pan with non-stick cooking spray.

○ In a small saucepan place apple cider, vinegar, margarine, olive oil, lemon juice, sugar, cinnamon, nutmeg, salt and cayenne pepper. Warm over low heat 3 to 5 minutes.

○ Place sweet potatoes, butternut squash, carrots and raisins in prepared pan.

○ Pour warm sauce over vegetables.

○ Cover tightly with aluminum foil. Bake at 375° for 1 hour and 30 minutes or until vegetables are soft. Serve immediately.

○ This sweet vegetable dish has a bit of a kick from the cayenne pepper and goes well as a side dish with Roasted Turkey (page 143).

Carrot Muffins

½   (10-ounce) package shredded carrots

1   (4-ounce) jar carrot baby food

1   teaspoon baking powder

1   cup flour

2   eggs

1   teaspoon lemon juice

¾   cup canola oil

2   tablespoons honey

1   teaspoon vanilla

1   cup sugar

1   teaspoon salt

○ Preheat oven to 350° F.

○ Line cupcake tins with paper holders.

○ In a large bowl, place all ingredients and mix well to combine.

○ Spoon mixture evenly into cupcake holders and bake for 20 to 25 minutes.

○ Allow to cool slightly and serve warm or at room temperature.

○ For a lower-calorie version, substitute applesauce for some or all of the oil and use egg substitute in place of the eggs.

PREP: 5 minutes

COOK: 30 to 40 minutes

CHILL: none

YIELD: 6 servings

Butternut Squash Soufflé

2   (10-ounce) packages frozen
      butternut squash, thawed

2   eggs, beaten

½   cup flour

½   cup light brown sugar, packed

½   teaspoon cinnamon

¼   teaspoon nutmeg

      Maple syrup (optional)

○ Preheat oven to 350° F. Spray a 9-inch
  round baking dish with non-stick cooking spray.

○ In a medium bowl, place squash, eggs,
  flour and sugar. Mix well.

○ Pour mixture into prepared baking dish.
  Sprinkle with cinnamon and nutmeg.
  Drizzle with a little maple syrup if desired.

○ Bake, uncovered, at 350° for 30 to 40
  minutes, until set and edges are slightly
  golden. Serve warm or cold.

Thank you, Abby (not my sister-in-law
Abbie, but my sister's friend Abby)
for this delicious, melt-in-your-mouth
soufflé that really is like dessert right
at the meal.

Also try baking this in a 9-inch frozen
piecrust.

Champagne Sweetened Lentils

2   cups lentils, rinsed

3 ½ cups water

¼   cup golden raisins

¼   cup raisins

2   tablespoons olive oil

¼   cup champagne or white wine

¼   cup maple syrup

1   teaspoon garlic powder or
     2 teaspoons prepared minced garlic

2   teaspoons salt

○ Mix all ingredients in a medium saucepan. Bring to a boil, uncovered, over medium-high heat.

○ Reduce heat to simmer. Cover and cook for 45 minutes to 1 hour or until lentils are tender but still hold their shape, and liquid is absorbed.

○ Transfer to a dish and serve immediately.

This is a great side dish for Roasted Turkey (page 143) or Roasted Cornish Hens (page 135).

Cran-Apple Crunch Kugel

PREP: 4 minutes

COOK: 45 minutes

CHILL: none

YIELD: 8 servings

1   (21-ounce) can apple pie filling

2   cups fresh or frozen cranberries

4   tablespoons sugar

4   tablespoons light brown sugar

1   cup flour

½   cup margarine, cut into chunks

1   teaspoon cinnamon

- Preheat oven to 375° F. Spray a 9-inch round baking dish or deep pie plate with non-stick baking spray.

- Place apple pie filling and cranberries in prepared dish, mix to combine and smooth into an even layer.

- In a small bowl, mix together sugars, flour, margarine and cinnamon until crumbly. Sprinkle over apple-cranberry mixture.

- Bake, uncovered, at 375° for 45 minutes or until crumbles are golden brown. This is best served right out of the baking dish.

Nobody will suspect you didn't spend half an hour peeling and slicing apples! The fresh, tart cranberries will totally throw them off, and they're the perfect balance to the supersweet pie filling.

205

Corn on the Cob

10 cups water
4 large ears corn on the cob
Margarine (optional)
Salt (optional)

- Place water in a 6-quart stockpot, cover and bring to a boil.

- Shuck the corn; remove the husk and silk (remove stubborn silk under cold running water) and break or cut off any remaining corn stalk.

- Once the water is boiling, add the corn, cover, turn off heat and let stand 3 to 5 minutes.

- Use tongs to remove corn.

- Serve with margarine and salt on the side, if desired.

I have great childhood memories of eating corn on the cob. My mom had those little corn-shaped picks we used to stick in either end of the corn to hold it while we ate. And my grandfather never ate it straight from the cob. Instead, he slowly and methodically sliced it off the cob. My sister and I used to drool, watching him, and after we quickly ate our portions he would generously share his sliced corn off the cob with us. It didn't work if my mom sliced it off the cob for us and put it on our plates. Somehow, the corn from Uputzi's plate tasted better, and we only wanted that.

Don't add salt to the water because it toughens the kernels.

Desserts:
My List of "I Never"

Allow me to share a little lesson in "I never." It's quite all right to say past tense nevers – things like "I never went skydiving" or "I've never been good at science." But I learned the hard way that future "nevers" are traps. Nowadays, in addition to eating my cooking, I am eating my words as well.

I was never going to: Cook. Quit my job. Skip my honeymoon. Not have makeup on when my husband gets home. Bake ("never, ever!")

So now: I wrote a cookbook (obviously) and quit my "super glamorous" TV job to stay home with my daughters. As for my fantasy month-long honeymoon on a tropical island (so exotic that its name is unpronounceable)? Never happened. Though after two years of marriage, we did take a two-day trip to scenic Huntington, Long Island.

The last time I wore a face-full of makeup was my wedding, I think. I once heard some elderly women giving tips for a fulfilling marriage. They swore that putting on makeup for your husband every day was the key to lifelong bliss. And I believed them. It's a good thing Hubby never heard their rules.

And guess what? Baking challah every week is one of my joyous pastimes. Don't get too excited, though. My best ever challah is not a 15-minute recipe; it's closer to 5 hours from start to finish. But I discovered that the prep time for baking most other things really is 15 minutes or less! Some you don't even have to bake; you freeze them. Who knew?

It turns out that baking my own sweet, satisfying dessert is more fun than buying one – and it often tastes better, too. I learned a lot about it from my sister-in-law Abbie. She may as well be a professional baker. She uses ingredients I never heard of and can whip up a dessert faster than I can turn on the oven. She has the cutest way of color-coding her desserts to fit the occasion, too: shades of blue if a boy was born, pinks and purples

if it's a girl. Her Shabbos treats are worth waiting for all week.

So here I am, trying to be like her. But I'm all inspiration, with no talent and no time. So I worked over her recipes, along with those graciously donated to me by my other food-savvy relatives, to make baking and desserting a lot easier for me – and for you. (In this book, desserting is not a capital offense.) Here and now, I confess to simplifying the prized recipes of our family's Perfect Pie Professional, Six-Braid Challah Queen, and Cookie Connoisseur who bakes the wickedest chocolate chip cookies ever!

They all think it's hysterically funny that Jamie – all-thumbs-in-the-kitchen-Jamie – actually gets a charge out of making and serving her own desserts. My unsuspecting guests have no idea how many tries it took till I got the recipes right; no concept of which ingredients I nixed because they were too much of a potchke; and above all, not the slightest notion of how many calories they're consuming. Some secrets are best left unrevealed.

Raspberry Twists

1   frozen puff pastry sheet (from a 17.3-ounce package), defrosted

2   tablespoons margarine, softened

½   cup seedless raspberry jam

1   tablespoon cinnamon sugar, divided

○ Preheat oven to 350° F. Lightly grease a cookie sheet with non-stick baking spray.

○ Unfold puff pastry onto a flat surface.

○ Spread margarine on the puff pastry.

○ Spread jam in a thin layer, leaving a 1-inch border for rolling. Sprinkle with ½ tablespoon cinnamon sugar.

○ Roll as for a jelly roll, secure seam side down and cut into 18 thin slices.

○ Place slices on prepared cookie sheet. Sprinkle remaining cinnamon sugar over slices.

○ Bake at 350° for 20 minutes, or until puffed and golden brown.

○ Serve warm or at room temperature.

Suggested Wine: Hagafen 2005 Potter Valley White Riesling.
The exotic fruit of this Riesling (mango and papaya) will work in perfect harmony with the raspberry jam in this recipe.

These look and taste like perfect little bakery cookies. For a twist on these twists, top each cookie with 1 tablespoon of non-dairy whipped topping and sandwich them.

Pinwheels

PREP: 11 minutes
COOK: 20 minutes
CHILL: none
YIELD: 18 cookies

1   frozen puff pastry sheet (from a 17.3-ounce package), defrosted

1/4   cup liquid marble or liquid chocolate paste

2   tablespoons brown sugar, packed

2   tablespoons confectioners' sugar

1   tablespoon unsweetened cocoa powder

1/2   teaspoon freeze-dried instant coffee granules

1/2   teaspoon cinnamon

1   tablespoon walnuts, ground medium fine

Additional confectioners' sugar, for dusting (optional)

○ Preheat oven to 350° F. Lightly grease a cookie sheet with non-stick baking spray.

○ Unfold puff pastry sheet onto a flat surface.

○ Spread a thin layer of liquid marble or liquid chocolate over pastry sheet, leaving a 1-inch border for rolling.

○ In a bowl, mix sugars, cocoa, coffee granules, cinnamon and ground nuts.

○ Sprinkle powdered mixture over liquid marble or chocolate.

○ Roll as for a jelly roll, place seam side down and cut into 18 thin slices. Place slices on prepared cookie sheet.

○ Bake, uncovered, at 350° for 20 minutes, or until puffed and golden brown.

○ Serve dusted with confectioners' sugar, if desired.

This recipe was adapted from one given to me by champion baker Rebbetzin Heller. I consider it a mark of her infinite kindness that she shared her trade secrets with a novice like me. She taught me about ingredients like liquid marble. Just look for it in the supermarket baking section with the other chocolate products. Now I give people the recipe and say, quite matter-of-factly, "and of course, you use liquid marble," as though it's something I've known about my entire life.

You can easily turn these pinwheel cookies into a yummy strudel. After rolling like a jelly roll, brush with a lightly beaten egg. Bake at 375°F for 35 minutes, until golden brown. Cool for 30 minutes, sprinkle with confectioners' sugar and slice into 8 thick pieces.

Tea Biscuit and Sorbet Tower

2   (4.2-ounce) packages of tea biscuits
3   pints sorbet in 3 different colors
    (such as raspberry, mango and
    coconut), softened
    Strawberry sauce (optional)

○ Place layer of tea biscuits in bottom of an
  8-inch square baking pan. Spread 1 pint
  of sorbet over biscuits, to cover completely.

○ Alternate layers of biscuits and sorbet,
  ending with sorbet.

○ Freeze for at least 4 hours or overnight.

○ Drizzle with berry sauce over top or
  around the tower on the plate before
  serving, if desired.

This recipe came via my Aunt Judi, via my cousin Adina, via her neighbor Tamar. It's perfect as a dessert after a heavy feast or as a finisher to the meal leading into the Yom Kippur fast.

For a Fourth of July picnic, you might construct a red (raspberry or strawberry), white (coconut) and blue (blueberry) sorbet tower.

Jelly Roll

PREP: 14 minutes
COOK: 14 minutes
CHILL: none
YIELD: 8 servings

4	eggs, at room temperature
1	cup granulated sugar
½	teaspoon salt
1	cup flour
1	teaspoon baking powder
1	teaspoon pure vanilla extract
1½	cups strawberry or raspberry jelly or jam
½	cup confectioners' sugar, divided

○ Preheat oven to 350° F. Line an 11 x 16-inch jelly roll pan with wax paper lightly greased with non-stick baking spray.

○ In the bowl of an electric mixer, beat eggs for about 1 minute. Gradually add in granulated sugar, beating for another 4 minutes, until fluffy and pale yellow in color. Add salt and beat for 15 to 30 seconds.

○ Fold in flour and baking powder gently but thoroughly, being careful not to deflate the eggs. Fold in vanilla extract.

○ Spread batter in prepared pan and bake at 350° for about 14 minutes until the center springs back when lightly touched (check after 12 minutes).

○ Immediately turn out onto a clean, damp dish towel sprinkled with ¼ cup confectioners' sugar. Peel paper from bottom of cake and roll in the towel. Unroll and spread with jelly or jam and roll again inside the towel.

○ Remove towel, put cake on a plate, seam side down, and sprinkle with remaining confectioners' sugar. Slice and serve.

215

In this book, you will find several rolls that are made in the same way as a jelly roll. Here is the real thing. It's a great way to use up leftover jam and jelly.

If you forget to take the eggs out ahead of time, just place them in a bowl of warm water for 3 to 5 minutes.

PREP: 15 minutes

COOK: 12 minutes

CHILL: none

YIELD: 20 cookies

Chocolate Chip Cookies

²/₃   cup margarine, softened

½   cup granulated sugar

½   cup light brown sugar, packed

1   egg

1   teaspoon pure vanilla extract

1   cup flour

½   cup whole wheat pastry flour

½   teaspoon baking soda

¼   teaspoon salt

1   (10-ounce) bag chocolate chips

○   Preheat oven to 350° F. Liberally grease two cookie sheets with non-stick baking spray.

○   In the bowl of an electric mixer, beat together margarine, sugars, egg and vanilla until smooth and creamy. Set aside.

○   In a large bowl, whisk together flours, baking soda and salt.

○   Combine margarine mixture with flour mixture and add chocolate chips; stir until well blended.

○   Drop 10 heaping tablespoons of cookie batter onto each prepared cookie sheet, about 1-inch apart.

○   Bake at 350° for 12 minutes or until cookies are firm in the center.

○   Allow to cool on the cookie sheets before removing with a spatula and serving.

These are my sister-in-law Debbie's absurdly famous cookies. The original version is from *Second Helpings, Please* by Norene Gilletz and Harriet Nussbaum, and published by Gourmania Inc. The book and recipe are more than 35 years old, but worth digging into the archives for. Debbie usually quadruples the recipe and makes little cookie goodie bags for her friends. It's gotten to the point where she actually serves them to her guests before the meal, because no one can wait till dessert time!

Whole wheat flours can go rancid very quickly. If possible, store in a sealable plastic bag in the freezer and only keep for about a month after opening. To test whether whole wheat flour has spoiled, sample a little on the tip of your finger. It should not taste sour.

PREP: 5 minutes

COOK: 4 minutes

CHILL: none

YIELD: 4 servings

Homemade Chocolate Fondue

½   cup unsweetened cocoa powder

¾   cup sugar

½   cup margarine

½   cup liquid non-dairy creamer

*For dipping,
choose any or all of the following:*

Fresh fruit

Dried fruit

Marshmallows

Brownies

Soft chewy cookies

○ Sift cocoa through a fine mesh sieve.

○ In a saucepan, over medium heat, combine cocoa, sugar, margarine and non-dairy creamer, stirring continuously for 4 minutes or until heated through.

○ Pour cocoa mixture into a fondue pot or bowl for dipping.

○ Surround with selected dipping treats and serve with toothpicks.

My mom didn't hit the stove too often while my sister and I were growing up, but fondue was her forté. She always wanted to make sure we ate enough fresh fruits and vegetables, and fondue was her way of luring us to a fruit salad. She would spend hours washing berries and cutting up all sorts of exotic fruits along with apples, pears and bananas.

Suggested Wine: Hagafen 2005 Napa Valley Late Harvest Zinfandel. Chocolate fondue will be fairly heavy on the palate. Late Harvest Zinfandel will match the cocoa, but its fruit will also pair well with the fruit dipped in the chocolate.

Ambrosia Soup

PREP: 8 minutes

COOK: none

CHILL: 2 hours

YIELD: 8 servings

2   (8-ounce) containers non-dairy frozen ready-to-whip liquid topping, thawed

1   (4-ounce) can mandarin oranges, drained

1   (12-ounce) container frozen strawberries in sauce, thawed

1   (15-ounce) can pineapple tidbits, drained

1   (15-ounce) can sliced mango, drained, cut into bite-sized pieces

1   (15-ounce) can sliced peaches, drained, cut into bite-sized pieces

½   cup coconut flakes

- Place topping, oranges, strawberries and sauce, pineapple, mango and peaches in a large glass bowl. Stir gently to mix.
- Chill in refrigerator for 2 hours.
- Sprinkle coconut flakes on top. Serve.

This is a non-traditional variation on classic ambrosia. It looks fabulous presented in a glass bowl and ladled out at the table. I like to serve it as a fruity sidekick to rich chocolate desserts.

Applesauce Cake

PREP: 5 minutes
COOK: 1 hour
CHILL: none
YIELD: 8 to 10 servings

3   cups flour

1¹⁄₂ cups sugar

²⁄₃   cup canola oil

1   (12-ounce) jar applesauce

2   eggs

2   teaspoons cinnamon

1   tablespoon baking powder

¹⁄₈   teaspoon salt

1   teaspoon pure vanilla extract

2   teaspoons cinnamon sugar

¹⁄₂   cup non-dairy whipped topping

○ Preheat oven to 350° F. Lightly grease a 9 x 13-inch cake pan with non-stick baking spray.

○ In the bowl of an electric mixer, combine flour, sugar, oil, applesauce, eggs, cinnamon, baking powder, salt and vanilla. Mix on medium speed until well combined, about 2 minutes.

○ Pour into prepared pan. Sprinkle with cinnamon sugar.

○ Bake at 350° for 1 hour, or until a toothpick inserted in the center comes out clean.

○ Serve warm or at room temperature with a dollop of non-dairy whipped topping.

Strawberry
Shortcake Trifle

PREP: 5 minutes
COOK: none
CHILL: 2 to 3 hours
YIELD: 8 servings

225

1 (16-ounce) prepared pound cake, cut into 1-inch cubes, divided

2 (12-ounce) packages frozen strawberries in syrup, thawed, divided

2 (8-ounce) containers non-dairy whipped topping, divided

- Crumble 4 cake cubes to resemble coarse crumbs. Set aside.

- Place half the remaining cake cubes in the bottom of a glass trifle bowl.

- Spread one package of strawberries in syrup over the cake layer.

- Cover with 1 container non-diary whipped topping, spreading to edges.

- Repeat layer with remaining cake, strawberries and whipped topping.

- Sprinkle reserved cake crumbs over top.

- Chill in refrigerator for about 2 to 3 hours before serving, but no longer than 4 hours, because whipped topping will begin to liquefy.

Thanks to Dani, my sister-in-law's sister-in-law who's also a friend of mine, I learned of a new kosher ingredient on the market: non-dairy (already whipped) whipped topping. Such a time saver in so many recipes! Now I don't have to whip up the non-dairy liquid topping when all I want is a simple dollop or layer of whipped "cream." This recipe, for example, might not have been possible within the time constraints of this cookbook if not for Dani's find. I won't be over-dramatic and call her a life saver; let's just call her a time saver. And that's the ultimate compliment in my book!

Decorate the top with fresh sliced strawberries if you like. Or, for a different flavor note, use lemon pound cake.

Suggested Wine: Hagafen 2005 Potter Valley White Riesling.
Gooey strawberry shortcake needs a wine that will cut through its whipped topping. The high acid and summery fruits in this Riesling will do the job beautifully.

Pumpkin Pie

PREP: 7 minutes
COOK: 45 minutes to 1 hour
CHILL: 2 hours
YIELD: 16 servings

226

4   eggs, lightly beaten

1   (29-ounce) can pumpkin puree

1   (8-ounce) container non-dairy frozen
      ready-to-whip liquid topping, thawed

1   teaspoon ground cinnamon

1   teaspoon ground ginger

1   teaspoon ground nutmeg

½   teaspoon ground cloves

¾   cup light brown sugar, packed

2   (9-inch) frozen prepared piecrusts
      Vanilla non-dairy ice cream
      (optional)

○ Preheat oven to 400° F.

○ In a large bowl, place eggs, pumpkin and
  topping. Mix well.

○ In a small bowl, mix together cinnamon,
  ginger, nutmeg, cloves and sugar. Combine with pumpkin mixture.

○ Mix until smooth. Divide in half and pour
  into each piecrust.

○ Bake at 400° for 15 minutes; reduce
  heat to 350° and bake for 30 to 40 minutes or until firm. Cool 2 hours at room
  temperature.

○ Serve each slice with a scoop of non-
  dairy ice cream, if desired.

The summer before I went to college,
my family moved to North Miami
Beach. I was so unaccustomed to the
heat and humidity that I longed for
the fall season up north. I became
obsessed with pumpkin pie, maybe
because I associated it with cool, crisp
autumn days. Now it's no longer a
seasonal favorite. In our home, pumpkin pie is always in season!

Suggested Wine: Hagafen 2005 Estate Bottled Napa Valley White
Riesling Pumpkin pie is all about spice – and this Riesling has it galore.
Its litchi and cherries will work perfectly with the nutmeg and ginger.

"Forgotten" Macaroons

2   egg whites

¾   cup sugar

¼   teaspoon salt

1   teaspoon vanilla

2   cups coconut flakes

○ Preheat oven to 350° F. Lightly grease two cookie sheets with non-stick baking spray.

○ In the bowl of an electric mixer, beat egg whites for approximately 9 minutes or until they stand in stiff peaks, then continue to beat for another 3 to 4 minutes as you slowly add the sugar. Don't worry if the sugar doesn't dissolve completely.

○ Beat in salt and vanilla. Stir in the coconut.

○ Scoop heaping teaspoons of mixture and drop onto prepared cookie sheets.

○ Bake at 350° for 20 minutes and then turn oven off. Leave macaroons in oven overnight or for about 9 hours.

○ In the morning, remove macaroons from cookie sheets. Store in sealable plastic bags or in airtight containers until serving.

○ These macaroons, the quintessential Passover confection, are called "forgotten" because you leave them in the oven overnight. They cook in the retained heat. You can dip them in high-quality melted dark chocolate if you like.

○ Oven temperature is crucial here; it's like the "Three Little Bears" and needs to be just right. So you may want to invest in an oven thermometer in order to be precise.

Puff Pastry
Apple Purses

PREP: 12 minutes
COOK: 45 minutes
CHILL: none
YIELD: 4 servings

1/3   cup chopped nuts

1/3   cup raisins

1/3   cup light brown sugar, packed

2   medium baking apples, such as Rome or Cortland, peeled, cored and halved

4   frozen puff pastry squares (from a 20-ounce package), defrosted

1/8   teaspoon cinnamon

2   teaspoons honey

1   pint vanilla non-dairy ice cream (optional)

- Preheat oven to 350° F. Lightly grease a 9 x 13-inch pan with non-stick baking spray.

- In a bowl, mix the nuts, raisins and brown sugar. Set aside.

- Place 1 apple half, skin side down, on a puff pastry square. Pastry should be pliable enough to twist.

- Fill apple cavity with nut mixture, approximately 1/4 cup per apple half.

- Bring pastry up and around the apple half to cover. Twist the corners together so it looks like a drawstring purse.

- Sprinkle with cinnamon and drizzle with honey. Repeat with remaining ingredients.

- Place in prepared pan.

- Bake, uncovered, at 350° for 45 minutes or until apples are soft. A sharp knife inserted into an apple should slip out easily.

- Serve each with a scoop of non-dairy vanilla ice cream, if desired.

This dessert is like a present. You discover a treat all wrapped up in puff pastry: a soft, sweet apple. This is a lighter dessert and pretty low in calories if you skip the non-dairy ice cream. After all, it's your apple for the day. Or you could serve it as a complement to a richer dessert if you want to give people two options.

For a change of pace, substitute dried cranberries or dried blueberries for the raisins.

Suggested Wine: Hagafen 2005 Estate Bottled Napa Valley White Riesling. The raisins, brown sugar, cinnamon and honey require a wine to accent their sweetness. The Napa Valley Riesling will do so with aplomb.

One Bowl Amazing Chocolate Cake

2   cups flour

2   cups sugar

1   (3.3-ounce) package Osem Instant Chocolate Pudding Mix

$^2/_3$ cup unsweetened cocoa powder

$1^1/_4$ teaspoons baking powder

1   teaspoon baking soda

1   cup liquid non-dairy creamer

$^1/_2$ cup canola oil

$^1/_2$ cup mayonnaise

3   eggs

2   teaspoons vanilla

○ Preheat oven to 325° F. Lightly grease a Bundt pan with non-stick baking spray.

○ In the bowl of an electric mixer, whisk together flour, sugar, pudding mix, cocoa, baking powder and baking soda.

○ Add non-dairy creamer, canola oil, mayonnaise, eggs and vanilla. Beat at medium speed for 2 minutes.

○ Pour into prepared Bundt pan.

○ Bake at 325° for 45 to 50 minutes, or until a skewer inserted in the center comes out clean. Let cool in pan about 20 minutes. Loosen sides and center with a knife and invert onto a serving plate

Everyone has a go-to recipe for a one-bowl cake. Here's mine. It's a combination of three or four recipes and, yes, I think it's the best. Or should I say amazing? The mayonnaise and pudding really moisten the cake, and you'll also score beauty points with presentation because, as I always say, anything baked in a Bundt pan will impress your guests. It's like a self-decorated cake.

For a glaze, place 1 cup chocolate chips and $^1/_2$ cup non-dairy frozen ready-to-whip liquid topping, thawed, in a small saucepan. Heat until melted and drizzle over cake.

Suggested Wine: Hagafen 2005 Napa Valley Late Harvest Zinfandel. Chocolate cake needs to be paired with a wine that will accent the chocolate, and the sweet strawberry jam of this Late Harvest Zinfandel will do just that.

PREP: 7 minutes

COOK: 40 minutes

CHILL: none

YIELD: 8 servings

Chocolate Liqueur Pie

1   cup light brown sugar, packed

2   tablespoons granulated sugar

$^1\!/_2$ cup margarine

$^1\!/_4$ cup cornstarch

2   eggs

3   tablespoons chocolate liqueur,
     or to taste

1   cup crushed walnuts

1   cup chocolate chips

1   (9-inch) frozen prepared piecrust
     Non-dairy whipped topping
     (optional)

○ Preheat oven to 350° F.

○ In the bowl of an electric mixer, place
  sugars, margarine, cornstarch, eggs and
  chocolate liqueur. Beat for about 2 to
  3 minutes.

○ Fold in nuts and chips.

○ Pour into piecrust.

○ Bake, uncovered, at 350° for 40 minutes,
  until top is golden brown.

○ Serve warm or at room temperature, with
  non-dairy whipped topping, if desired.

I love *The Mothers' Center Cookbook*, even
though it's older than I am. My mother-
in-law gave me the cookbook, which was
put together by a group of working moms
from Hicksville, New York. She edited
it, and my husband is one of the kids on
the cover. How could I not love it?

The *Mothers' Center Cookbook* version
of this recipe calls for bourbon. I wouldn't
have trusted myself behind the wheel
after one bite of that pie, so we changed
it to chocolate liqueur and reduced the
amount. If you love bourbon or are feeling especially daring, try 1 tablespoon
bourbon instead of the liqueur. It provides
a seriously strong dessert experience.

Use 1 tablespoon pure vanilla or chocolate extract in place of liqueur for a
non-alcoholic version.

PREP: 11 minutes

COOK: 45 to 55 minutes

CHILL: none

YIELD: 8 servings

Chocolate Chip
Banana Cake

3	cups flour
1	tablespoon baking powder
2	cups sugar
1/2	teaspoon salt
3	large ripe bananas
2	eggs
2	sticks margarine, melted
1	teaspoon vanilla
1/2	cup soy milk
1	cup chocolate chips

- Preheat oven to 350° F.
- Grease Bundt pan with non-stick baking spray.
- In a bowl, mix flour, baking powder, sugar and salt.
- In another bowl, mash bananas. Mix in eggs, margarine, vanilla and soy milk.
- Gradually combine dry ingredients with wet ingredients. Mix for about 2 minutes. Be careful not to overmix.
- Stir in chocolate chips and pour into prepared Bundt pan.
- Bake at 350° for 45 to 55 minutes, until a skewer inserted in the cake comes out clean. Let cool in a pan about 20 minutes.
- Loosen sides and center with a knife and invert onto a serving plate.

Serve with a scoop of non-dairy vanilla ice cream, banana slices and drizzled chocolate syrup.

Peanut Butter Chocolate Chip Mousse Pie

PREP: 11 minutes

COOK: none

CHILL: 4 hours

YIELD: 8 servings

1   cup unsweetened cocoa powder

1/2   cup light brown sugar, packed

3/4   cup sugar

2   (8-ounce) cartons non-dairy frozen ready-to-whip liquid topping, thawed

1/2   cup smooth peanut butter

2   tablespoons margarine

1   tablespoon pure vanilla extract

1/2   cup chocolate chips

1   (9-inch) prepared chocolate graham cracker piecrust

○ In the bowl of an electric mixer, place cocoa, sugars, topping, peanut butter, margarine and vanilla. Beat for about 3 to 4 minutes, until thoroughly blended.

○ Fold in chocolate chips.

○ Spoon into graham cracker piecrust.

○ Freeze at least 4 hours. Let soften slightly in refrigerator or at room temperature before slicing.

Suggested Wine: Hagafen 2005 Napa Valley Late Harvest Zinfandel. This is a full-bodied dessert, so it needs a a wine that can stand up to its big mouthfeel. The oak and sweetness of the Zinfandel harmonize with the creaminess of the mousse.

My sister Shoshana came home from her friend Sarah's house raving about this dessert. Her recipe was revised to make it quicker, and thank goodness none of the taste was sacrificed.

To make this dessert look extra fancy, create chocolate shavings by using a grater or vegetable peeler on a chocolate bar. Sprinkle shavings over the top. Or decorate with chocolate syrup.

Chocolate Quesadillas

PREP: 3 minutes
COOK: 3 minutes
CHILL: none
YIELD: 4 wedges

2   (8-inch) flour tortillas
2   tablespoons peanut butter
2   tablespoons Marshmallow Fluff
2   tablespoons chocolate chips

- Heat a large skillet on medium low heat.
- Place tortillas on a flat work surface.
- Spread 1 tablespoon peanut butter, 1 tablespoon Fluff and sprinkle 1 tablespoon of chips on each tortilla.
- Fold each tortilla over to form a semicircle.
- Spray both sides of quesadillas with non-stick cooking spray.
- Put both quesadillas in skillet for 1 to 2 minutes.
- Flip over for another 1 to 2 minutes until brown and crisp.
- Slice with pizza cutter or knife. Serve immediately.

In France and Denmark, bread and chocolate is an after-school treat. Sometimes it's bread and Nutella. So this would have to be the Mexican-kosher-Jewish version of bread and chocolate. Once your family and guests taste these quesadillas, you won't be able to keep them coming fast enough.

If you prepare these in advance, keep them warm in the oven at 200°F.

Chocolate-Covered Matzohs

PREP: 10 minutes
COOK: 2 minutes
CHILL: 2 hours
YIELD: 8 matzohs

239

8   slices matzoh

1   (10-ounce) bag semisweet
     kosher-for-Passover chocolate chips

2   tablespoons margarine

○ Place matzoh on 2 cookie sheets lined
  with wax paper.

○ Place chocolate chips and margarine in
  microwave-proof bowl and heat in microwave until chocolate is almost melted,
  about 2 minutes. Check and stir every
  20 seconds until completely melted and
  well combined.

○ Spread melted chocolate mixture over
  matzoh, using a spatula. Let cool at room
  temperature, about 2 hours.

○ When chocolate has hardened, stack matzohs between layers of wax paper. Store
  in airtight containers. Before serving,
  break into smaller pieces, about the size
  of a cookie.

Kosher for Passover food is very expensive and this recipe and Forgotten
Macaroons (page 227) are big money
savers. I'm not only into saving time,
but money, too.

To make super impressive chocolate-
covered matzohs, double the amount of
chocolate chips and margarine. When
the matzohs are cool and chocolate has
hardened on one side, turn over and
coat the other side.

PREP: 10 minutes
COOK: 4 minutes
CHILL: 3 hours, 30 minutes
YIELD: 4 to 6 servings

Lemon Ice

2   cups water
1¼   cups sugar
⅛   teaspoon salt
2   teaspoons lemon zest
½   cup fresh-squeezed lemon juice

○ In a saucepan, bring water to a boil and stir in sugar and salt until dissolved. Cool.

○ Add lemon zest and juice.

○ Pour into 2 metal ice cube trays with dividers removed, or a metal bowl, or a 9-inch square baking pan and freeze.

○ After about 1½ hours, remove from freezer and rake a fork through the ice, to fluff it up.

○ Return to freezer for about 2 hours.

○ Remove from freezer about 20 minutes before serving, so ice is easy to scoop.

241

An easy way to zest a lemon is to use a grater with small holes and grate the peel off the lemon directly over a bowl to catch it. Be sure to use only the colored part of the peel. 1 lemon yields approximately 1 tablespoon zest. Zest is best grated fresh and used immediately.

The Crust of the Matter

I know you turned to this page eager to find a 15-minute super shortcut to challah preparation. Okay, you caught me. I confess that these recipes are not quickies. Think of them as a bonus. When you're successful baking your own challah, you may consider yourself a graduate of my *The Bride Who Knew Nothing* cooking course.

A hallmark of Jewish cuisine, challah is eaten at every Shabbos and festival meal, except Passover, of course. The tradition is to set out two challahs to commemorate the two portions of manna that fell for the Israelites every Friday during their 40-year sojourn in the desert. The double portions were enough to sustain them well through the Sabbath, when no manna fell and none was gathered.

Challah recipes are as varied as can be, but common to all are the warm memories they create. Anyone who has entered a kitchen while challah is baking will forever recall that tantalizing aroma. And the magic carries over to Friday night, when the rich sheen of the challah crust in the candlelight suggests the wonderful meal to come.

My friend Basha (sister-in-law to Monet, whom I've told you and told you and told you about) is responsible for the basic recipe provided here. It was inspired by her mentor, Goldie, and a wonderful teacher, Rebbetzin Miller. Basha went on to develop the recipe with her own tricks and I took a cue from her and tweaked it ever so slightly. But the heart of the recipe is still the same, as is the method, which I believe is what makes it such a success.

The recipe in this chapter can be adapted many ways, and I've included a few variations to get you started. The chocolate chip idea comes from my sister-in-law Debbie and my neighbor Galit. They happen to be the best of friends, so I'm not sure whether Galit got it from Debbie, or Debbie got it from Galit. In any case, do we really need a reason to stick chocolate into bread?

Raisins are a sweet option that my mom loves. And the totally untraditional idea of adding Craisins came from Monet (there she is again!), who's a totally untraditional chef. Once she even dreamed up a garlic and sun-dried tomato whole wheat challah. So as you can see, once you've mastered challah, the sky's the limit.

To braid or not to braid: That's the question for many new challah bakers. It's not so difficult to create the traditional six-braid challah, provided you have someone to show you the way. Back when I was trying to learn this technique, Basha's 7-year-old daughter, Malka, deftly taught me how to do it! The point is that I've found that this lesson needs to be taught in person. Any description I've read or diagram I've tried to follow has left me frustrated, with a big knot and not a beautiful braid. If you can't find a Malka, round challahs and pull-aparts are an easy alternative. They're traditionally used around the High Holidays or any time the baker is in a rush.

Try the recipes on the following pages and don't be afraid. If I can do it, you can, too!

Challah

PREP: 1 hour
COOK: 35 to 45 minutes
CHILL: 2 hours
YIELD: 4 large challahs

3½ tablespoons kosher salt

1 (6-pound) bag high-gluten flour, divided

2½ cups light brown sugar, packed

3 (¼-ounce) packets active dry yeast

4 egg yolks

6 cups warm water

¾ cup canola oil, divided

2 whole eggs, lightly beaten

½ cup sesame seeds

½ cup poppy seeds

○ Place salt in a huge plastic bowl.

○ Reserve 6 cups flour, and pour remaining flour into bowl.

○ Add sugar, yeast and egg yolks.

○ Make a well in the middle and slowly pour warm water into the well. Make sure the water is not too hot. It should be no warmer than you would use for a baby's bath.

○ Start kneading ingredients together and add half the oil.

○ For the next 15 to 20 minutes, knead, adding the remaining oil slowly during that time, and adding flour, about 4 cups, as needed to create a workable dough. Dough shouldn't be too sticky and also should not be dry. It should become one cohesive mass.

(Recipe continues on next page)

Challah freezes well. After cooling completely, wrap in aluminum foil and freeze for up to 1 month. When you're ready to use a loaf, just pop it, completely frozen and still in the foil, into a preheated 325° F oven for about 30 minutes, or until you can squeeze it and feel that it's soft.

○ When dough is smooth and satiny, rub a little oil over the top and cover bowl with a kitchen towel. Place covered bowl in a medium plastic garbage bag and place open ends of the bag loosely underneath the bowl, trapping in air.

○ Place in a warm spot and let rise for 1 hour or until doubled in size.

○ Punch dough down and knead, flipping it and releasing any air bubbles. Cover again, using the towel and the bag, and let rise ½ hour. Punch down again, and let rise for another ½ hour.

○ Punch down and divide dough into 4 equal parts.

○ Liberally spray four (9-inch) round disposable baking pans with non-stick cooking spray and set aside.

○ Preheat oven to 375° F.

For Pull-Apart Challah:

Use some of the remaining 2 cups of flour to dust a flat surface. Place 1 piece of dough on it. Play with the dough a bit, squeezing out any air bubbles. Separate into 8 equal parts. Roll each part into a round ball, adding flour as needed to keep it from being too sticky. Don't use too much flour; a little sticky is fine.

Place one ball in the middle of the prepared pan and surround with remaining balls. Don't worry if they don't touch. They will rise into each other while baking. Set aside.

For Round Challah:

Use some of the remaining 2 cups of flour to dust a flat surface. Place 1 piece of dough on it. Play with the dough a bit, squeezing out any air bubbles. Then roll the dough into a long, thick rope, adding flour as needed to keep it from being too sticky. Don't use too much flour; a little sticky is fine.

Place one end of the rope up against the edge of the prepared pan and coil it, ending in the middle. Set aside.

○ Repeat either method with remaining dough and 2 cups flour so that you have 4 challahs.

○ Brush challahs with beaten egg and sprinkle with a combination of poppy and sesame seeds.

○ Bake at 375° F for 35 to 45 minutes, until challah tops are dark golden brown. Allow to cool slightly before slicing. Serve while still warm. Once the challah has been sliced, you can store the slices in sealable plastic bags for about 4 to 5 days.

For all challah variations below do not sprinkle with sesame or poppy seeds.

Chocolate Chip Challah
At step 3, add 2 cups chocolate chips.

Maple Syrup and Craisin Challah
At step 3, add 2 cups Craisins and ⅓ cup maple syrup.

Cinnamon Raisin Challah
At step 3, add 2 cups raisins and ¼ cup cinnamon sugar. Before placing in oven, brush with egg and sprinkle ¼ cup of cinnamon sugar over tops of challahs.

Challah Garlic Bread

6   thick slices challah
4   tablespoons margarine
3   tablespoons prepared crushed garlic
½   tablespoon dried parsley flakes
½   tablespoon onion powder

o   Preheat oven to 425° F. Lightly grease
    a cookie sheet with non-stick cooking
    spray.

o   Place challah on prepared cookie sheet
    and spread evenly and liberally with
    margarine.

o   Sprinkle bread slices with crushed garlic,
    parsley flakes and onion powder.

o   Bake at 425° until slightly toasted and
    edges are crisp.

We love to dip our garlic bread in the
sauces of many pasta dishes, such as
Creamy Ziti (page 306), and Linguini
and Tomato Sauce Florentine (page
308), as if we weren't eating enough
carbs already!

You can use other breads for this recipe,
such as white, sourdough or even whole
wheat.

Shopping Like an Expert: Shake, Rattle and Roll

The finer points of picking produce and other shopper's challenges

To me, turning down the produce aisle of the supermarket is venturing into a veritable twilight zone. As I stand there, dumbfounded, the woman next to me is expertly tapping, shaking, listening and examining specimen after specimen of melons and fruit. To my horror, everyone in this pseudo-universe is doing it! They squeeze and tap with grim determination and utter confidence, sorting through the stock until they find perfection.

I don't speak the language and I don't know the customs. Should I casually press the melon grooves or sing to the apples and listen for an echo? Truth be told, I quickly fill my bag and skedaddle out of the aisle, leaving the experts to their studies.

While I was contemplating writing this cookbook, I went out to dinner with my Aunt Rachel, the one who was born a sublime cook. I'm sure that as a toddler, she skipped the blocks and coloring books and went straight to whipping up a batch of linguini and tomato sauce Florentine. I told her I was considering including a section on how to choose produce, not because I know how, but precisely because I don't. There must be plenty of others like me, I reasoned. Brimming with glee, Aunty bubbled, "What a great idea! You can explain to people the difference between a male and female eggplant..." and then I just tuned her out. My head was nodding and my mouth was turned upward in some sort of agreeable grin, but my mind was going crazy. Male and female eggplants? Who knew? Are the female eggplants more sensitive? Are the males tougher-skinned? Would they rather get lost than ask for directions?

As it turned out, I discovered that my husband knew more about this mystery than he initially let on. Over the first few months of our marriage, like all newlyweds, we did everything together – even the food shopping. We'd take turns, one of us pushing the cart, the other holding the list. So sweet, right?! Hubby tried to teach me the finer points of picking produce, but somehow the lessons got mired in my brain. I remember something about pressing the top (or was it the bottom?) of the cantaloupe. It's supposed to be soft, or was it hard? There was some shaking involved, I believe. Apples should be hard, avocados soft, but that may depend on when you plan to eat them: today, tomorrow or two days from now. Help!

And my agonies didn't end when I escaped the produce aisle. If you're like me, picking out meat is one of the scariest moments of the shopping trip. There are so many choices, different cuts and varying prices that a novice shopper could stand in front of the meat section, eyes glazed, for hours.

I tend to stare into the fish showcase in the same stupor. Truth be told, I have no nose for fish, no idea how to pick out the best fillets. Do I have to go for the most expensive one on display? What's the difference between farm raised and wild salmon, anyway? Did the farm fish graze on inferior grass and the wild one spend too much time in the principal's office?

What about all those kosher brands of groceries? How is a girl to know which ones she'll want to serve to guests and which should only be given to a ravenous 2-year-old? For that matter, which products are new to the kosher scene and would really impress the boss, and which ones are old hat?

So many questions, so little time to become the perfect shopper: So I turned to Supersol kosher supermarket in Lawrence, New York, my favorite food emporium, and asked their experts.

What I found out will amaze you. The produce manager gave me the lowdown on choosing fruits and veggies; the meat manager patiently explained how to bring home the right cuts for the right price, for every recipe. He even gave me such esoteric information as the difference between lamb chops and baby lamb chops and why some ribs are called first cut and some are called second cut (betcha don't know). The fish manager gave me an earful on mahi mahi and some good, solid, fishy advice. And the manager of the grocery section told me everything I need to know about kosher food trends.

I knew I wouldn't remember all these revelations, so I dutifully recorded every word of our interviews. Check them out on the following pages. The information I got solves the mysteries, ends the jitters and makes shopping fun!

To read extended versions of these interviews, please visit www.quickandkosher.com, where you'll also find free recipes, food and lifestyle articles and much much more.

"If you shake a melon, you're just bruising it."

Picking Produce:
There Are No Seasons Anymore!

An interview with Steven Beck, produce manager at Supersol

Q: I've always wanted to ask this: What's the difference between a male eggplant and a female eggplant?
A: Ha! My family has been in this business for generations. My grandfather and my father laughed when people asked about it. Maybe the farmers know.

Q: So it doesn't matter?
A: Nope.

Q: Okay then, what do I look for when picking out an eggplant?
A: If you have two eggplants that are the same size, take the lighter one. Lower weight means there are fewer seeds in it.

Q: Why do various kinds of cucumbers have different tastes? And how do Kirby cucumbers differ from the Persian and Israeli varieties?
A: Kirby cucumbers are American grown. They are smaller than the big cukes and have less water, so they have more taste. The other small, tasty varieties are Persian and Israeli cucumbers. They're both thinner than the Kirbys and seedless.

Q: Which tomatoes have the best flavor?
A: "Best" is a matter of opinion. Holland cherry tomatoes have excellent flavor, though grape tomatoes are more popular. Different color tomatoes don't necessarily taste better, but they're good for presentation. If you want a really special-looking tomato, try little "teardrop" tomatoes. They're expensive and highly perishable, but gourmets love them.

Q: Are gourmet varieties of fruits and vegetables more perishable?
A: No, it just seems that way. At times of high demand, prior to holidays for instance, the turnover is rapid. Once demand slacks off, gourmet produce may be in the store longer, so it won't be as fresh when you buy it.

Q: What about the different varieties of lettuce? Which are considered gourmet?
A: Depends on how gourmet you want to get! There's mâche, red oak, frisée and radicchio. Other options are chicory, endive and arugula, which each have a slight bite.

Q: Do all onions make you cry?
A: Actually, no. Vidalia onions don't make you cry. They're also sweet and have no bitter aftertaste, which is why a lot of cooks favor them.

There's a lot of variety in onions: Spanish – also called Bermuda onions – are large, round and easier to cut. Pearl onions look nice in many dishes. Leeks and scallions are in the onion family, too.

Q: What do you call a regular onion?
A: Is this a joke?

Q: No! Seriously, what is it called and how should you pick one?
A: It's called a globe onion. Look for nice, smooth skin and regular shape, so it will slice evenly.

Q: Describe a ripe avocado.
A: Avocados come in green and start to turn black as they ripen. They should be tender to the touch, but not too soft. If you buy a hard one, it takes two to three days to ripen.

Q: So when I bring home fresh produce, should it go into the fridge or stay out?
A: Up to you. I like most things at room temperature, but certain items will last longer in the fridge. Apples, for example, will stay crisper if you refrigerate them. When you shop, ask the fruit manager if the item should be refrigerated.

Q: Should I keep produce in the plastic bag?
A: Never! It doesn't breathe in there. Get produce out of the plastic right away.

Q: Okay, the big question: How should I choose a melon? Should I shake it?
A: If you shake a melon, you're just bruising it. Press the end of the melon. It should have a little bit of give, not too much. Look for skin texture. On a honeydew or Crenshaw melon, look for brown honey spots coming out of it. Veins and honey spots on the skin mean there's good texture inside.

For a cantaloupe, pick one with no scars, tears, bruises or blemishes in the skin, and the netting should be fairly well defined.

Q: With so many colors of grapefruit to choose from, how can I pick a perfect one?
A: White grapefruits are almost a thing of the past! Most people prefer the pink and red ones. Look at the texture of the skin. A grapefruit that's too large with a thick skin is hollow inside. I like them a little soft to the touch – they're sweeter.

Q: Apples come in so many varieties. Which are best for baking?
A: For baked apples, use Rome or Cortland. Granny Smith apples are good for pies. They should be firm, even for baking. Watch the skin. A bruise means there's a black spot inside. If you want to know how an apple is supposed to taste, go to a farm in the fall and get them right off the tree.

Q: Is it best to eat fruits in season?
A: There are no seasons anymore! We get produce from all over the world, year-round, so it's not as much of an issue as it used to be. If you're talking about local produce, however, it's great to buy it when it's fresh and plentiful.

Q: Since we do get a lot of produce from other places in the world, are there health concerns?
A: Foreign produce has gotten better and better. But consumers should know that a lot comes from South America, where laws regarding pesticides are different from those in the U.S. Make sure you wash produce very well, no matter where it grew.

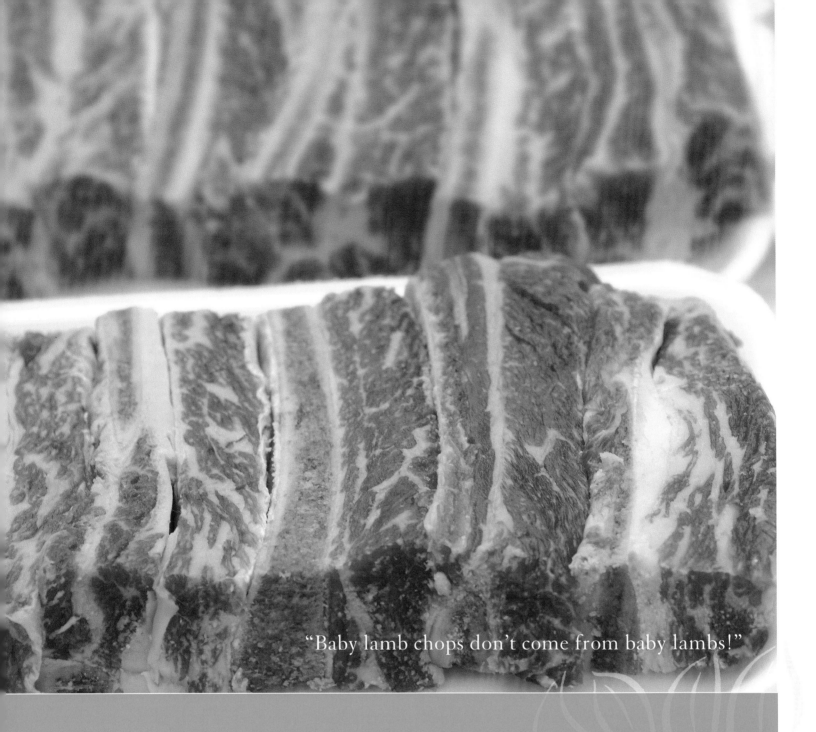

"Baby lamb chops don't come from baby lambs!"

Meat Matters:
An Enlightening Meating

An interview with Levi Baron, manager of the meat department at Supersol

Q: Why do different butchers call the same cuts of meat by different names?

A: It depends on your background and it's a regional thing. For example, New York has special cuts like New York minute steaks. Also, certain butchers may call cuts by different names to differentiate themselves. Remember that the back half of the cow is not eaten by kosher consumers in the U.S., so many "upscale" cuts, like filet mignon, are actually not kosher. Our customers still want to see those names, so we use the glamorous monikers for different cuts.

Q: So what parts of the cow do we use?

A: We use the front half of the cow called the forequarter. This includes the 12th rib and forward, chuck, neck, shoulder and breast – that is basically the whole forequarter.

Q: The French roast – that melt-in-your-mouth, scrumptious piece of meat – is from what cut of the cow?

A: It's from the top chuck. Here at Supersol, we call it brick roast, but ask any butcher anywhere for top chuck French roast and you'll always get what you're looking for.

Q: Since the French roast is very expensive and definitely a splurge item for most shoppers, what are the alternatives?

A: French roast, rib roast, first cut corned beef brisket and regular brisket are great for holidays and entertaining the boss or your in-laws. For a good meat meal that isn't as extravagant, try London broil, minute roast, silver tip roast, square cut roast, chuck eye, and top of the rib. Incidentally, "Prime" and "Choice" are terms used to designate grades of meat. Prime is the best and Choice is the next level.

Q: You mentioned "first cut brisket." What is meant by "first" and "second cut"?

A: On a first cut, considered the better of the two, the eye is bigger, and the bone is smaller. On the second cut, the bone is longer and there's less meat. There are also first cut corned beef briskets, rib steaks, veal chops and even baby lamb chops.

Q: Baby lamb chops come from baby lambs, right?

A: Baby lamb chops don't come from baby lambs! They're called baby because they're smaller than the shoulder or round bone lamb chops. The meat on the baby lamb chops is the best, most tender meat on the lamb, in the same way first cut veal chops are the most tender cut of veal.

Q: What is veal, and why does it taste different from beef?

A: Veal is from a calf. The meat is very tender and lighter in color. It tastes different because the muscles are not formed the way they are in a mature cow.

Q: How about some tips on choosing and storing meat? How can you tell that you've found a good piece of meat?

A: It should be red and marbleized (fat inside the meat). The fat separates the meat, and helps it melt in your mouth. Veal should be pink, not dark. (It's not marbleized like beef.)

Q: What should you avoid when choosing meat?

A: Black color, darkening, green spotting. If the bone is turning black, but the meat looks okay, it was probably previously frozen, but that doesn't mean it's spoiled.

Q: How long will meat stay fresh in the refrigerator? The freezer?

A: Meat will last a few days in the fridge. If you have any doubts, smell it. A foul odor means it's not good. In the freezer meat can last for months. Just wrap it really well so there's no air, and seal it.

Q: We haven't discussed poultry yet. I've always wondered, are Cornish hens a particular species of hen?

A: No, they're baby chickens. In general, the size of the chicken has to do with its age when it is slaughtered and processed: A Rock Cornish hen weighs 1 to 1¾ pounds and can serve one person. Two-pounders can be cut in half to serve two; they have less fat and are more flavorful than older chickens. A broiler (your average chicken) weighs 3 to 3½ pounds. Pullets weigh 3½ to 5 pounds and are great for soup.

Q: How can I tell if a chicken is fresh?

A: A good indicator is white skin color. If

the meat under the skin looks faded, not pink, it's not as fresh. Also, there shouldn't be too much liquid in the bottom of the tray.

Q: Let's talk about cooking! What is flanken and why is it used for chulent?

A: Any meat is good for chulent! Flanken is Yiddish for "sides of beef." It generally refers to a strip of beef from the chuck end of short ribs. It's sometimes favored for chulent because it's fatty and has bones, both of which give the chulent a really good flavor.

Q: Is there a formula for estimating how much meat I need per serving?

A: If it's the main course, you should allow about ¾ pound per person, because meat shrinks. If many other dishes are being served, you can allow approximately ½ pound per person.

Q: There are always other dishes being served, but I use ¾ of a pound per person anyway.

A: So does my wife. You probably have a lot left over.

Q: Yes, but I do it anyway because I'm always afraid I won't have enough.

A: So is my wife.

"If you smell fish in the house, you've overcooked it!"

Fish Food for Thought:
Something's Fishy Here

An interview with Dave Scott, manager of the fish department at Supersol

Q: What is the most requested fish in your display case?

A: Salmon by far. It can be prepared so many ways and it can be served cold or warm. Anything you do with it works.

Q: There seem to be a lot of categories of salmon. How do they differ?

A: The most readily available salmon is from Canada; it's a "farm fish." Alaskan salmon, the most common "wild fish," is phenomenally expensive and, in my opinion, doesn't really taste as good. In recent years, there's been some controversy over wild fish versus farm fish. But most authorities agree that whatever risks there are with a farm-raised fish, it still pays to eat it rather than pass it by entirely.

Q: What's the difference between tuna steak and the kind that comes in the can?

A: Canned white tuna is albacore and the chunk light is made from yellowfin. Fresh tuna steaks sold at the fish counter are yellowfin tuna.

Q: What kinds of white, flaky fishes are available?

A: The most commonly requested flaky fish is flounder, and for good reason. It comes in a range of sizes, adaptable to any recipe. The thinnest, smallest pieces fry very nicely. Larger pieces are best baked or broiled. There are approximately 30 types of flat fish. We call them all flounder here.

Halibut is also in the flaky fish family – think of it as a big, fat flounder. Usually cut as steaks, it's also available in fillet form or you can have it cubed as a mock scallop.

Tilapia is popular because it does well with any cooking technique. Then there's Chilean sea bass, a thick, fatty fish that people tend to love or avoid completely. It's pricey though, as is Dover sole (another type of flounder). The expensive fish are not usually stocked, but you can order them.

Q: Does good fish have to be expensive?

A: People think you have to spend a fortune to get good fish, but Nile perch provides very good value. It has a mild taste and soft texture. It's also a healthful fish and very good baked or broiled. By the way, Nile perch usually costs half as much as flounder and is a good substitute to use in any flat fish/flounder recipe.

Q: What makes a fish popular?

A: It's funny. People have a perception about fish – they want it light-colored, except for salmon. Mackerel is very healthful, but not very popular because it has a bluish tinge. The same goes for Boston bluefish.

Q: Does a strong fish odor have anything to do with the freshness of the fish?

A: Fresh fish will not have an odor. (The exception is whitefish, which has a specific aroma.)

Q: How long can raw fish be kept in the fridge?

A: Salmon and tilapia have a long shelf life – three to four days – though to preserve the flavor, I recommend not leaving it more than two to three days. Any other fish from Supersol or another reputable fish counter should last two to three days in the fridge.

But watch out for real McCoy mahi mahi, which comes from the waters of Hawaii. It must be super fresh: It's not that mahi mahi spoils sooner; it just loses its taste. We don't carry it here because, as far as I'm concerned, they can't get it to the market fast enough to preserve its true flavor.

Q: What's your opinion of fresh versus frozen?

A: Pre-packaged frozen fish from your store's freezer aisle is less expensive. An alternate option is to have your fish guy freezer pack fresh fish from the counter for you. My method of choice is tightly wrapping the fish in plastic wrap and then over-wrapping it with either aluminum foil or wax paper. This will help ensure that no air gets into the fish, because when air gets in, that's when it gets freezer burn. Wrapped like this, the fish could last one to two months in the freezer.

Q: Any tips on cooking fish?

A: Most types of fish cook very rapidly. Overcooking compromises its nutritional benefits. Generally, cooking a fish at 350°F for 20 to 25 minutes is all you need. Once you start smelling fish in the house, it's overdone! It means the fats are starting to sizzle and the fish is drying out.

Q: How has gefilte fish changed over the years?
A: Gefilte fish is just seasoned, ground fish. Sometimes eggs, matzoh meal, and/or onions are added. Whitefish, pike and mullet are most often used today. Carp used to be popular, though the color is darker and it has a distinctive flavor. It's no longer used by most people.

If you like gefilte fish made from fresh fish, you can ask your fish store to grind it for you. The prepared frozen loaves are good, too. Your grandmother slaved over her gefilte fish for hours because she had to clean it and grind it herself. You can do it in a jiffy.

"Convenience is a big, big thing.
Even flip-top tuna cans are more popular!"

Grocery Goldmine:
Everything's Kosher Now!

An interview with John Litras, manager of the grocery department at Supersol

Q: What's kosher nowadays that wasn't before?

A: Now they have just about everything kosher! Nabisco cookies went kosher a few years ago – now half their line is kosher. About five or six years ago, the Asian foods took off. Italian companies became kosher, too, particularly their specialty pasta sauces. Their research showed there's a market for these items among kosher consumers.

Q: Do these specialty items – like ethnic food ingredients – sell well?

A: It depends on what locale you're in. In some places, they do extremely well and in others they sit on the shelf. You have to know your clientele. Every community seems to have its brand preferences, too. In some neighborhoods, only the Jewish companies will sell; in others, the big name brands do better.

Q: What's one of the most expensive specialty items sold at Supersol?

A: Pomegranate juice! I can tell when a new recipe has been printed in Jewish newspapers and calls for an unusual ingredient, like pomegranate juice – suddenly I have 150 people coming in here asking, "Do you have any pomegranate juice?" Then the item becomes a staple in the store.

Q: What specialty foods are most requested?

A: Asian items with name brands that have good kosher certifications are the most popular.

Q: Are Jewish brands more expensive than name brands?

A: Not necessarily. Big name brands are usually more expensive and sometimes don't sell as well because a lot of them are dairy.

Q: What's most important to today's shopper?

A: Convenience is a big, big thing. Even flip-top tuna cans are more popular! Prepackaged, quick and easy items sell fast. In today's world, disposability is very important, too. Disposable foil tins and paper goods are on most shopping lists.

Q: How has the Passover market changed over the last 20 years?

A: How hasn't it changed? Things nobody ever dreamed would be kosher for Passover are available now. You can get pizza mix, muffin mix and mustard, to name just a few. The best sellers are still candy and chips. Listen, you can find just about anything you want kosher for Passover – but I don't guarantee how it's going to taste!

"Wine is special because it's alive!"

Wine 101:
Fruit of the Vine
An interview with Ernie Weir, owner and winemaker of Hagafen Cellars of Napa Valley,
producers of gold medal wine since 1979

I didn't know I married into a family of wine connoisseurs until shortly after the wedding. At that point I discovered that my new Uncle David was a collector of vintage wines and the proud owner of the Geller Family Wine Cellar. The truth is, I don't think Uncle David planned for his wine cellar to be anyone's but his own, but he gladly stores our wine collection now – proud that his nephew has followed in his footsteps.

Our life savings have gone into this wine collection, which my husband deems an investment. Now, I'm not against a sound investment, and I enjoy a good glass of wine as much as anyone, but I had sort of hoped we'd invest in a house. The way it looks now, we may one day have to move into Uncle David's wine cellar or build a house out of our used corks. No joke – Hubby actually saves them all in hopes of building something with them one day. Building things out of corks must be a total guy thing, because I just don't get it.

In any case, while I was writing this book, my connoisseur was appalled that I'd even consider writing about food without its natural companion. He convinced me that this feature was essential to the success of *Quick & Kosher*. I agreed. As a newly-minted Geller, I had to take wine very seriously. The only trouble was that I knew practically nothing about it.

So I turned to an expert for help: Ernie Weir, owner and winemaker of Hagafen Cellars of Napa Valley, California.

As you'll see, Ernie's knowledge and candor are remarkable. Not only did he explain the mysteries of wine making, tasting and buying, he combed through the recipes and holiday menus of this book to expertly match the award-winning Hagafen wines with what I hope will be our award-winning dishes! His effort will save you a great deal of agony trying to figure out which wine pairs well with each dish. Now, when you get to the store, don't despair if you can't find the exact vintage (i.e. year) that Ernie has recommended. He explained to me that one of the benefits of being a small winery is that Hagafen has the ability to craft "house styles" for their wines. This means that while there may be slight differences, the overall style of, for example, a Hagafen Cab or Pinot, does not change drastically from year to year. Go with the same varietal and you'll still get a great match.

Naturally, Ernie is enthusiastic about grapes grown in Napa Valley. But the general information he imparts applies to wonderful wines that come from Israel and other locations as well. The interview you will find on the following pages can be used as a quick reference guide by novice wine devotees like me, but even those in the know will find Ernie's tutorial fascinating. Think of it as Wine 101 and Advanced Wine Tasting rolled into one course – an accomplishment worthy of a toast!

Q: How is wine produced?

A: Wine is fermented grape juice. Placing the fermented juice in oak barrels will impart different flavors and aromas to the wine. Placing the wine in stainless steel barrels will not. These are stylistic choices that winemakers make. The basic process itself is very simple: Grow grapes, pick them, crush them, add yeast and you'll have wine. The rest is artisanal crafting (at least it is at Hagafen!).

Q: What is a varietal?

A: "Varietal" refers to wines made chiefly from one variety of grape and which, therefore, take on the dominant characteristics of that grape.

Q: In layman's terms, then, what are the differences between the following varietals: Cabernet, Merlot, Bordeaux, Pinot Noir, Syrah and Zinfandel?

A: Cabernet is king for a reason – it ages the longest, provides the widest and deepest range of flavors, and with good acid structure to balance alcohol and fruit, it can age for many, many years in good storage conditions. However, California Cabs are, by and large, made to be drunk "young," hence their very fruit-forward profile.

Merlot is usually used as a blending wine in France, as a way of smoothing out Cabernet Sauvignon, but in California, it's very often bottled as a single varietal. Whereas Cab is big and bold, Merlot is subtle and nuanced.

French Bordeaux wines are made from the careful blending of different varietals. "Left Bank" wines have Cabernet Sauvignon as the major varietal in their mixes; "Right Bank" wines have Merlot. Both versions of Bordeaux blends tend to have lower alcohol levels and higher acid than their New World counterparts. (This is all a factor of weather; the sun, specifically. We'll discuss more about grape-growing environments later.)

French Pinot Noir is produced in Burgundy, and many see it as the ultimate expression of the term *terroir* (i.e., reflective of the soil and climate in which it grew). California Pinots have a variety of styles, but in general, Pinot Noir is considered the most mutable of reds, its flavors food-friendly, but soft on the palate.

Syrah is the New World spicy wine, high in acid and a good food match. In France, these are known as Rhône blends because of the geographic location where they're grown.

Zinfandel is considered California's home-grown grape, but it's actually a transplant from Europe. It reaches a depth of spice in California heat, though.

Q: What do you mean by "acid" and why is it "good"?
A: When we say a wine has good acid we mean that there is enough acid in the wine to balance the fruit and alcohol, which is known as a wine having good structure. A balanced wine of any varietal dances on the tongue because its components work together and are not out of whack.

Q: I see. OK. Let's move on to the white wines: What's the difference between Chardonnay, Sauvignon Blanc, White Riesling and sparkling wine/Champagne?
A: Chardonnay is that most versatile of white varietals: There are literally dozens of styles. Oaked Chardonnays tend to be very woody, while the unoaked ones are usually much purer in their apple fruits. Secondary fermentation produces styles ranging from a hint of creaminess to very buttery wines.

Sauvignon Blanc is typically a high-acid wine,

sometime with hints of grassiness and other times with pure citrus or steely notes. Another technique is to "oak" the Sauvignon Blanc; hence the term "Fumé Blanc" to describe this style.

Riesling is perhaps the most underappreciated of white wines in the United States. These wines can age for 50 years or more – the white counterpart to Cabernet, if you will. Their combination of residual sugar and high acid makes them wonderful food wines.

Sparkling wine is just as varied as any other varietal. The best create the bubbles in the bottle over a period of time before being released to the market, sometimes stretching for more than seven years as they gather creaminess.

Q: Is it a rule that white wines should always be chilled?
A: Both white and red wines should be served cooler than what we think of as room temperature. Whites should be around 55 to 60 degrees, and reds should be 60 to 65 degrees. You want acid to balance against the alcohol, oak and fruit, and the cooler temperatures encourage that balance.

Q: So should white be in the fridge and red in a cool, dry place? What's the best way to achieve these temperatures for that perfect balance?
A: The easiest way is to store both in the fridge and simply allow the red a little time out of the fridge before you serve it.

Q: I've heard that wine should "breathe." How is this done and why is it necessary?
A: Oxygen is your friend when it comes to wine. It encourages the phenol compounds that make up so much of wine-tasting; 85 percent of tasting is with the nose, not the tongue. One easy way to let a wine breathe is to open it about an hour before you are going to drink it. If that's not possible, make sure you swirl your wine for a good two to three minutes.

Q: What does swirling do?
A: Swirling does two things: It lets you see the coloration and clarity of the wine, and it also allows the introduction of air to bring out the bouquet. Not swirling is like not adding salt to a steak – the extra ingredient that acts as a catalyst to your act of enjoyment.

Q: What does bouquet mean?
A: Bouquet is a fancy way of describing what you smell in a wine. The idea is that by oxygenating the wine, you "open up" the bouquet, like

a spray of flowers coming out of the glass.

Q: What does it mean when wine is described as dry?
A: That the level of residual sugar in the wine is less than about 0.4 percent by volume. Most wines have at least a little bit of residual sugar from incomplete primary fermentation, but our tongues generally can't taste that sweetness below the 0.4 percent threshold.

Q: Is there any benefit to sniffing the cork?
A: Sniffing, no. You should, however, feel the cork to see that it is moist. Look at it, too, to see that it's in good shape, without any obvious leaks up one side, etc. This tells you a little bit about the storage conditions of the wine, an especially important thing when having wine at a restaurant and paying the markup.

Q: Wine tasting seems to be an art. What is the proper way to taste test wine? Why do people spit out the wine after tasting?
A: The steps of tasting are fairly simple. Start by pouring about 2 ounces of wine into a glass (it should take up less than one-third of the glass). Look at the wine to make sure there are no obvious visual defects: Is the wine cloudy? Is it the wrong color for the varietal? A white wine that is brown is oxidized and won't taste good. A red wine should look purple if really young or shades of maroon as it starts to age. Burnt brown, unless in a really old wine, is a sign of oxidation (think sherry and you'll know what I mean).

Next, swirl the wine in the glass, with your hand covering the bowl to keep the bouquet in. Sniff deeply. What comes to mind? That's the bouquet. Now take a small sip and suck in a bit of air as you do so. This, too, helps to oxygenate the wine.

Run the wine throughout your mouth and over all parts of your tongue, especially underneath, which is very sensitive. After 10 or 15 seconds, spit the wine out. What flavors come to mind? Think about fruits – tropical and citrus for whites, red and black for reds. What did the oak add? Think about spices, like clove or vanilla or cocoa. How long does the taste last in your mouth? That's the wine's finish, and the longer, the better.

If you are only tasting one wine, go on to enjoy it. If you are tasting multiple wines, spitting is key because it helps to prolong palate fatigue and keeps the effects of the alcohol in check. You want to be as clear-headed as possible, particularly if you are tasting to purchase.

Q: For the average person who doesn't have a wine cellar: How do you recommend they store the wine they purchase?
A: Store wine in the darkest closet in the center of your home, as far away from light or temperature variations as possible. If the bottles are corked, they should be kept on their sides. Cork is made of plant cells – a type of bark, in fact – and like most living things, it needs to be kept wet in order for it to do its job.

We recommend purchasing at least two bottles (or more) of a wine you really like. Have one bottle while it's young, so you'll know where the wine started. Savor the others every couple of years so that you can see, feel and taste how that wine changes in the bottle over time.

Q: How can you tell if the wine you are buying has been stored properly?
A: Take a look at the wine bottle in profile. How far from the bottom of the capsule is the wine level in the bottle? (The capsule is the shrink-wrapped tube, usually made of tin, that covers the cork and extends several inches down the neck of the bottle.) Known as the "ullage," this is a measure of evaporation. Generally, more than half an inch or so of space says that the wine may have evaporated as a result of heat or a blown enclosure – a bad cork, for example. Also check to make sure there is no leakage onto the bottle from under the capsule – this is a sign of a wine that has been heat-damaged and thus bubbled up out of the bottle at some point.

Q: Why does wine improve with age?
A: Wine is special because it's alive! We use that term – aging – for a reason. Most good wines have a bright youth and then they begin to age, which adds complexity. They

also peak and begin a slow (and sometimes not so slow!), inexorable movement toward decline. Their power and fruit will dissipate, leaving not much, ultimately, besides some tannin and faint echoes of what was once in the bottle.

Q: Do all wines improve with age?
A: No. Most wine today is made to be very "fruit-forward," meaning to be drunk young. This, too, is a stylistic choice winemakers make. Hagafen is a little different. Yes, our wines can be consumed when young, but we craft them to age for a good, long while in the bottle. We try to give you the best of both worlds. And given the demand for our older library wines, most of which are no longer commercially available and only able to be purchased from us in Napa, I would say many others value that way of crafting wine, too.

Q: Once you've popped the cork on your wine, do you have to drink it all?
A: No, you don't have to drink it all. What needs to be done to preserve it depends on the varietal.

Wines with a good bit of sugar in them, like dessert wines, can be re-corked and then put into the fridge or left out. The sugar helps to protect the wine from oxidizing.

Sparkling wines need a sparkling wine enclosure, which helps to keep the pressurization intact so that the bubbles aren't lost for several days.

Non-sweet still wines can be dealt with two ways. If you know you are only going to have half a bottle, you can use a plastic water bottle that you've emptied and allowed to dry. As soon as you open the wine, pour half of it into the water bottle to the point where there is no air left at all and the wine is liter-

ally bulging at the top of the hole. Cap it tightly and store in your fridge; it should be good for several days. The other method keeps the wine in its bottle: Simply add in several spurts of a gas that comes in a canister – Private Preserve is what all the wineries in Napa use – and because the gases are neutral and heavier than air, the gas creates a barrier so that the wine will not oxidize.

Q: What is meant by the term wine country?
A: In part, it's a state of mind! Think of what the term connotes: a place of beauty, slower times, intense connections to the earth and to the climate. On another level entirely, it's a fact of law. Napa has been maintained in the face of increasing housing pressures by urban / rural boundaries wisely created many decades ago. Wine country is literally a place set aside for wine rather than strip malls or housing subdivisions.

Q: What distinguishes Napa Valley as a grape-growing region?
A: Terroir is a French term that is hard to translate. It means, literally, everything that is around the grapes: the soil, the rootstock, the weather, the sun, the climate, the way of trellising the vines, the oak in the barrels. Napa soil is just different than any other place on the planet – especially for big reds and nuanced whites.

Q: Is there a difference between the California grape and the French grape?
A: It's less about the grape than about the sun. France gets good sun maybe four times a decade, while Napa gets good sun (approximately) at least eight times a decade. Our wines are generally bigger and fruitier; theirs are sometimes more reserved and nuanced. It's not so much one versus the other, but what you prefer that day.

Q: Is there any real difference between kosher and non-kosher wines?
A: That depends on whom you ask. As with everything involving wine, it's all about perception. We have hundreds of medals and high scores on our wines because they've been tasted blind. We argue that good wine is good wine, and bad wine is – not worth drinking!

Q: Then why do kosher wines have a reputation for being inferior?
A: In the old days, kosher meant a syrupy, overly sweet wine, the only kind then available. If your only point of reference is a Concord grape sweet wine, you're going to think that kosher wines are inferior. But if you've kept up with the changes in the kosher wine scene, you know that today's kosher wines are as excellent as any other wines.

Q: Let's talk a little about entertaining and cooking with wine. First off, when I set my table, does the type of wine glass really matter?

A: Yes and no. Is it necessary to have many sets of glasses, one for each varietal? Probably not. But having a set of Bordeaux glasses, which are highly oblong in shape, and a set of Burgundy glasses, which are fatter and shorter, is a good idea. A third set would be for sparkling wine – very tall and thin, to show off the bubbles.

Q: As a general rule of thumb, what goes best with red meat? Chicken? Fish? Pasta? Dairy?

A: There are hundreds of years of debate on this question! Generally, bigger red wines (Cabernet, Merlot and Syrah) go with red meats because their fruit and oak match the ways red meats are cooked. Chicken, fish and pasta call out for lighter reds (Pinot Noir, some Merlots, some Zinfandels or Sangiovese) or high-acid whites (Sauvignon Blanc and some Chardonnays). Dairy can be matched with lighter reds (Pinot Noir) or lower-acid whites (Chardonnay).

Q: How about some guidelines for what to serve with appetizers and desserts?

A: Sauvignon Blanc and Riesling are great for aperitifs or appetizers. They have a hint of sugar and good acid to spark the taste buds into awakening in preparation for the meal to come. Dessert is always tricky. Try late harvest Zinfandels or port wines with chocolate, and Rieslings that have residual sugar or Sauterne-style dessert whites with fruit.

Q: What does wine do when added to a recipe? Should cooking wine or a higher grade of wine be used? What do you suggest I use when a recipe calls for red or white wine?

A: Generally, adding wine to a dish adds layers of complexity. You need to make sure you cook off the wine, though, because the alcohol can interfere with the dish. Just add the wine sooner rather than later, so that the alcohol has time to evaporate. And throw out your cooking wine! If you wouldn't drink it, why cook with it? A good rule of thumb is to use the same wine in the preparation of the dish that you plan to serve with it. A nice harmony will develop as a result.

For more information about Hagafen Cellars and its wines, visit their website at www.hagafen.com. And to bring Hagafen wines into your life on a regular basis, check out their wine clubs at www.prixhagafen.com.

Hagafen

Reserve
2006
Napa Valley
Pinot Noir

 Estate Bottled
Fagan Creek Vineyard
Block 38

From Extra Cheese to Extra Cream:
Pizza, Pasta and Other Dairy Pleasures

I married a pizza connoisseur. If it were up to my husband, we would have pizza for breakfast, pizza for lunch and pizza for dinner. He knows every pizza shop in town, including their baking cycles, so we can get there when the pie is just coming out of the oven. And he has the shops' quality ranked in his own mental dining guide, based, I suspect, on the agility of the bakers and the frequency of their turnaround.

He's quite convinced that no one can properly duplicate "pizza shop pizza" at home. Everyone knows that great pizza is made only by guys dressed in white, covered with flour and specks of sauce. The pie has to go in and out of the oven on one of those wooden pizza paddles, or whatever they're called. So I won't offend the likes of Hubby by saying that my homemade pizza stands a chance against the professional kind. *But,* between you and me, mine is pretty darn good. In addition to a standard quickie, pita pizza, I've put an exotic pizza recipe in this chapter, invaluable when you want a twist on the familiar or get tired of standing on line at your favorite pizza joint.

Another personal favorite is pasta, and all things cheesy. I love these dishes on the well-done side, bubbly and brown. Our home is well-known for our ziti. I'm calling it "our" ziti when it's really my husband's ziti. His secret ziti recipe was one of the many precious things he brought to our marriage, along with some old furniture, which he called "antiques." Our side table, which I really didn't care for, once belonged to his grandfather. There was a chest of drawers, which I really, really didn't care for, that once had a home in his uncle's room. Then there was a roll-top desk, which I really, really, really didn't care for, that had been his brother's. He also came with a trunk full of

tchotchkes, a huge dumbbell (bigger than me, but I'm smarter), some unusual magnets and 47 T-shirts.

But the ziti recipe – now that was something worth framing. It has become one of my/his – okay, *our* – signature pieces. Friends have asked me for it, both the recipe and the ziti itself. So I'll pass along this scrumptious recipe to you, along with all of Hubby's little tips that go with it.

In case your mouth isn't watering yet, take a look at my desserts, made with sour cream, butter, puddings and heavy cream. They are so luscious, you won't mind the ramifications. As my grandmother always said, you can eat everything and anything as long as it's in moderation. Of course, she was a thin woman who always had candies in her purse and could eat a bar of halvah, one bite at a time, over the course of a week. So I'm not sure we can trust her on this.

SOUPS AND STARTERS ▶

Creamy Corn Soup

2   large potatoes, peeled and cubed

1   large onion, peeled and diced

3   (11-ounce) cans sweet yellow corn
      Niblets, not drained

3   cups whole or skim milk

³/₄   teaspoon ground nutmeg

1   teaspoon kosher salt

1¹/₂ cups heavy cream
      Minced fresh chives, for garnish
      (optional)

○ Place potatoes, onion and corn in a
  4-quart stockpot.

○ Add milk, nutmeg and salt; bring to a
  boil over medium-high heat, stirring frequently, being careful not to burn milk.

○ Reduce heat and simmer for 30 minutes,
  or until potatoes are tender and fully
  cooked. Keep heat low so that milk
  doesn't burn.

○ Add cream and heat through.

○ Ladle into bowls. Garnish each bowl
  with about 1 teaspoon minced chives,
  if desired.

When I was expecting my daughter,
Aunt Tamara bought me the sweetest
little cookbook called *Healthy Cooking,*
part of the Cookshelf Series from Par-
ragon Publishing. It languished on my
kitchen shelf for more than a year, until
I started writing this book. It was the
inspiration for so many recipes, including this rich and creamy soup.

Warm bowls are a nice touch for soup
and pasta. Warm them in the microwave,
in an oven at low heat or by pouring hot
water in them and drying just before
serving.

PREP: 12 minutes

COOK: 50 minutes

CHILL: none

YIELD: 6 to 8 servings

Leek, Potato and Tarragon Soup

3	tablespoons butter
1	tablespoon olive oil
2	leeks (white and pale green parts only), sliced
1	small onion, chopped
4	garlic cloves, sliced
1	pound small red-skinned potatoes, quartered
5	cups hot water mixed with 4 tablespoons Osem Vegetable Soup Mix
$\frac{1}{4}$	teaspoon salt
$\frac{1}{8}$	teaspoon coarse black pepper
$\frac{1}{2}$	cup heavy cream
$\frac{1}{2}$	cup plain whole milk yogurt
2	teaspoons fresh tarragon, minced

○ Melt butter in a 6-quart stockpot over medium heat and add olive oil.

○ Add leeks, onion and garlic. Cook over low heat until leeks are tender, about 10 minutes.

○ Add potatoes and broth and bring to a boil.

○ Reduce heat and mix in salt and pepper. Simmer until potatoes are tender, about 30 minutes.

○ Add cream, yogurt and tarragon, and heat through.

○ Ladle into bowls and serve.

Thank you, Aunt Tamara, for this delicious soup recipe. Tarragon and leeks are the perfect complement to a potato soup. The red-skinned potatoes make a big difference here, too. They have a subtle, yet distinctive taste and bring another dimension to the soup.

Be sure to wash leeks very thoroughly. Cut off the root end and slit the leek down the middle. Pull the layers apart and wash well under running water. Grit and sand are unpleasant additions to a soup.

Mango Soup

4   ripe mangos, peeled and pitted
1   ripe banana, peeled
2   (8-ounce) containers plain yogurt
½   cup sugar, or sugar substitute
     to taste
     Sliced strawberries, for garnish
     (optional)

○ Combine all the ingredients in a blender and puree until smooth.

○ Chill in refrigerator for 1 hour before serving.

○ Ladle into chilled bowls and garnish with fresh sliced strawberries, if desired.

This makes a delicious smoothie, too! Whether you put it in a bowl as a cold soup or in a glass as a cooling drink, you'll want more!

In hot weather, cold soup is super satisfying. Chill bowls in the refrigerator before serving for a cool touch.

French Onion Soup

4   large onions, sliced
4   tablespoons butter
1   cup dry white wine
2   tablespoons flour
8   cups water
3   tablespoons Osem Onion Soup Mix
1   teaspoon salt
½   teaspoon black pepper
     French bread, sliced and toasted

○ In a 4-quart stockpot, sauté onions in butter over medium heat for about 8 minutes, or until caramelized to a nice golden brown, stirring frequently so they don't burn.

○ Add wine and continue to sauté for 2 to 3 minutes.

○ Slowly stir in flour.

○ Stirring to keep lumps from forming, add water, onion soup mix, salt and pepper; bring to a boil over high heat.

○ Reduce heat to low, cover and simmer for 1 hour and 30 minutes.

○ Ladle into bowls and place a piece of toasted French bread in each.

To me, the best part of French onion soup is eating it out of a soup crock with the melted cheese. Of course, lots of people love the onion soup as is – and this does happen to be a phenomenal recipe – but on this one, I'm an all-or-nothin' gal.

The traditional topping used for onion soup is Gruyère cheese. If you have trouble finding it, substitute Swiss cheese. Top the toast with a slice or two of cheese and broil for 3 minutes, until cheese is browned and bubbly.

PREP: 12 minutes
COOK: none
CHILL: none
YIELD: 4 servings

Mozzarella and Tomato Stacks

¼   pound fresh mozzarella, cut into
       8 (½-inch-thick) slices

2   plum tomatoes, cut into a total of
       8 thick slices

8   fresh basil leaves

2   tablespoons olive oil

1½   teaspoons balsamic vinegar

½   teaspoon crumbled, dried oregano

1   teaspoon salt

       Additional fresh basil, for garnish
       (optional)

○ Place 2 mozzarella slices on each of four
   individual plates or arrange on a serving
   platter.

○ Place 1 basil leaf on each mozzarella slice.

○ Top each with a tomato slice. Set aside.

○ In a small bowl, whisk together olive oil,
   balsamic vinegar, oregano and salt. Drizzle
   over tomatoes and mozzarella.

○ Serve at room temperature, garnished with
   additional basil leaves, if desired.

Suggested Wine: Hagafen 2004 Napa Valley Zinfandel.
The high acid of this Zinfandel will work well with the tomatoes in this
dish, while its slight sweetness will harmonize with the balsamic vinegar.

If you have extra basil, place it in a
large glass or pitcher of cold water in
the fridge. It will last 4 to 6 days if
you remove wilted leaves and change
the water occasionally. This tip also
works with other fresh herbs.

Caviar and Chive Cream Cheese

PREP: 8 minutes
COOK: none
CHILL: none
YIELD: 8 to 10 servings

1	(8-ounce) container whipped cream cheese
½	cup fresh chives, chopped
¼	cup ikura caviar (salmon roe)
30	pita crisps

○ Mix cream cheese and chives until blended. Using an ice cream scooper or the back of a spoon, mold into a smooth, circular mound in the middle of a flat serving platter.

○ Top with caviar.

○ Surround with pita crisps.

To keep one or two lucky guests from snagging all the dip, serve as individual towers for a visual impact that is truly amazing. Place a spoonful of the cream cheese between two crisps, top with another spoonful of cream cheese and a dollop of caviar. Serve 3 per person.

To create homemade pita crisps, split a pita and cut each half into 8 to 10 triangular wedges. Lay wedges in a single layer on a baking sheet and place in oven at 300° F for about 15 minutes.

Suggested Wine: Hagafen 2001 Napa Valley Brut Cuvée Sparkling Wine. What could be better than caviar and sparkling wine? The saltiness of the roe is a perfect contrast to the toasty bubbles of the Brut Cuvée.

Mexican Quesadillas

PREP: 6 minutes
COOK: 15 minutes
CHILL: none
YIELD: 6 servings

6   (10-inch) flour tortillas

3   cups shredded mozzarella cheese

1½   cups canned corn (from an 11-ounce can), drained

1½   cups canned black beans (from a 15-ounce can), rinsed and drained

1   ripe Hass avocado, peeled, pitted and sliced

½   cup prepared salsa

½   cup sour cream

○ Heat a 12-inch skillet over medium heat.

○ Spray a tortilla with non-stick cooking spray. Place it flat on heated skillet for 1 minute and flip tortilla over.

○ Sprinkle 1 cup cheese on the tortilla, followed by ½ cup each corn and beans and 4 slices avocado.

○ Place another tortilla on top to make a sandwich. Cover pan with lid.

○ After 1 minute, flip the quesadilla.

○ When the cheese has melted, remove quesadilla and place on a warm plate; repeat with remaining tortillas, vegetables and cheese.

○ Cut each quesadilla into 4 wedges. Top each piece with a dollop of salsa and sour cream before serving.

It is hard to find good kosher Mexican food. I got so tired of looking that I decided to make it myself. Quesadillas are a great light appetizer. You can fill them with almost anything. Try my Chocolate Quesadillas (page 237). You'll wonder how you ever survived without them.

Warm a plate in the microwave for about 1 minute, a good idea for this or any other time you need to keep something nice and hot.

PREP: 14 minutes
COOK: 15 minutes
CHILL: none
YIELD: 6 servings

Spinach Tidbits

1 (16-ounce) package chopped frozen spinach, thawed and drained

¾ cup grated parmesan cheese

1 tablespoon dried minced onion flakes

1 egg, lightly beaten

1 cup seasoned mini croutons

2 tablespoons butter, melted

1 tablespoon prepared crushed garlic

⅛ teaspoon Tabasco sauce

○ Preheat oven to 375° F.

○ Lightly grease a cookie sheet with non-stick cooking spray.

○ In a large bowl, place spinach, parmesan, onion, egg, croutons, butter, garlic and Tabasco. Mix well.

○ Shape spinach mixture into 1-inch balls using hands or a melon baller.

○ Arrange on cookie sheet spaced 1-inch apart.

○ Bake, uncovered, at 375° for 15 minutes, until croutons are slightly golden.

This recipe was adapted (okay, snatched) from my Aunt Rachel's recipe box. In my opinion, it's the perfect party food. Put it on an hors d'oeuvre table with some crudité (that's raw vegetables) and dip.

If you want to lighten up pre-party anxiety, you can prepare this a week ahead of time. The spinach tidbits can be frozen after step 6. Freeze them on the cookie sheet overnight. Do not thaw them before baking; just increase baking time by 20 minutes.

Smoked
Salmon Rolls

PREP: 15 minutes
COOK: none
CHILL: none
YIELD: 5 servings

4   Persian or Kirby cucumbers, peeled

1½   pounds smoked salmon, sliced very
       thin to yield 16 slices

1   cup cream cheese

¼   cup capers, drained

1   tablespoon lemon juice

1   Vidalia onion, thinly sliced

16   grape tomatoes, halved

2   lemons, cut into wedges

       Flat breads (optional)

- Slice cucumbers lengthwise into 4 sticks each, so that you have 16 sticks total.

- On a flat work surface, place 1 piece of salmon horizontally.

- In a small bowl, mix together cream cheese, capers and lemon juice.

- Spoon 1 teaspoon cream cheese mixture onto 1 end of salmon slice. Place 1 cucumber stick on top of the cream cheese lengthwise, using the cheese to secure it.

- Roll the salmon around the cucumber and cream cheese like a jelly roll. Salmon should create a wide belt around the middle of the cucumber stick.

- Repeat previous 2 steps with remaining ingredients.

- Arrange sliced onions around the edge of a platter with rolls in the center; scatter grape tomatoes over and around rolls as a garnish and add a few lemon wedges for squeezing over salmon. Serve flat breads in a basket if desired.

Suggested Wine: Hagafen 2001 Napa Valley Brut Cuvée Sparkling Wine Late Disgorge Brut. **Late Disgorge Brut is even toastier and yeastier than Brut Cuvée – it's a natural match for the salmon. Its slight sweetness will also pair with the Vidalia onions and cucumbers.**

Have fun with appetizer presentation. It's a chance to use your creativity, even a touch of whimsy, to put a twist on this smoked salmon opener.

To make it really festive, use the green part of a scallion, tied as a bow, to secure each salmon roll.

SIDES AND SALADS ▶

Baked Cheesy Vegetable Crocks

4	celery stalks, chopped
16	grape tomatoes, halved
1	(15-ounce) can sweet yellow corn Niblets, drained
4	scallions, diced
$\frac{1}{2}$	teaspoon celery salt
$\frac{1}{4}$	teaspoon white pepper
4	(1-ounce) garlic and herb soft cheese triangles
$\frac{1}{2}$	cup plain yogurt
$\frac{1}{4}$	cup heavy cream
4	tablespoons grated parmesan

○ Preheat oven to 400° F.

○ Evenly divide celery, tomatoes, corn and scallions among four 7-ounce ramekins.

○ Sprinkle with celery salt and white pepper.

○ In a small bowl, mix cheese, yogurt and heavy cream until smooth; spoon 3 tablespoons of the mixture into each ramekin.

○ Top each dish with 1 tablespoon parmesan.

○ Bake, uncovered, at 400° for 30 minutes until hot and cheese has formed a crust. Serve warm.

○ You can serve these deliciously cheesy vegetable crocks straight out of the ramekins. It's another *Healthy Cooking* adaptation.

293

Cheese Quiche

1	cup half and half
4	eggs
$\frac{1}{8}$	teaspoon salt
$\frac{1}{8}$	teaspoon nutmeg
$\frac{1}{4}$	teaspoon pepper
2	tablespoons flour
$\frac{1}{2}$	cup shredded cheddar cheese
$\frac{1}{2}$	cup shredded havarti cheese
1	(9-inch) frozen deep-dish piecrust
$\frac{1}{2}$	cup shredded mozzarella cheese

○ Preheat oven to 350° F.

○ In a large bowl, whisk together half and half and eggs.

○ Add salt, nutmeg, pepper, flour, and cheddar and havarti cheeses. Mix well.

○ Pour into piecrust. Sprinkle mozzarella cheese on top.

○ Bake at 350° for 1 hour or until firm in center when pressed lightly with finger.

295

This is a basic light and fluffy cheese quiche recipe. It lends itself easily to variations. Try sauteing an onion or sliced mushrooms, or adding broccoli, spinach, or even some red peppers for taste and color. Use your imagination and have fun!

Macaroni Cheddar Salad

1   (1-pound) box elbow macaroni, cooked according to package directions

1   cup (4-ounces) cheddar cheese, cut into $\frac{1}{4}$-inch cubes

1   large celery stalk, diced

$\frac{1}{2}$ cup frozen green peas, thawed

$\frac{1}{2}$ cup packaged shredded carrots

$\frac{3}{4}$ cup light mayonnaise

$\frac{3}{4}$ cup sour cream

1   teaspoon celery seed

1   teaspoon garlic powder

$\frac{1}{2}$ teaspoon salt

Israeli (Mediterranean) pickles packed in brine, diced (optional)

○ Mix all ingredients in a large bowl until well combined.

○ Refrigerate for 2 hours before serving.

Suggested Wine: Hagafen 2005 Napa Valley Sauvignon Blanc.
The grassiness from the celery will find its ideal mate in this Sauvignon Blanc as it has a hint of freshly cut hay. Its high acid will also cut the mayo and cheese in the dish.

This is a great picnic salad. Add tuna, sliced hard boiled eggs or chunks of different cheeses for a heartier version. All you need now is a wicker picnic basket, a great wine (see Hagafen suggestion) and a guilt-free afternoon off.

PREP: 12 minutes
COOK: none
CHILL: none
YIELD: 6 to 8 servings

Goat Cheese Walnut Salad

2   (5-ounce) packages mixed
     field greens

1½   cups dried cranberries or Craisins

1   small red onion, thinly sliced

1   (5.5-ounce) log soft fresh goat
     cheese, crumbled

1½   cups walnuts

For Dressing:

2½   tablespoons red wine vinegar

1   tablespoon Dijon-style mustard

½   tablespoon fresh thyme, finely
     chopped

7   tablespoons olive oil

½   teaspoon salt

¼   teaspoon pepper

○ Mix greens, cranberries and onion in
  large salad bowl.

○ Sprinkle cheese and walnuts over salad
  mixture.

○ For dressing, mix vinegar, mustard and
  thyme in small bowl.

○ Gradually whisk in olive oil; season with
  salt and pepper.

○ Toss dressing with salad immediately
  before serving.

Exotic yet easy dishes seem to be Aunt
Tamara's specialty. I'm grateful to her
for introducing me to this marvelous
salad. Goat cheese is so soft and creamy
and has a distinctive flavor that is special in salads, sandwiches and even pizza.

To bring out a nice roasted nutty flavor,
place the walnuts in a shallow baking
dish and roast them in the oven for
10 minutes at 350° F.

Pasta Niçoise

1 (12-ounce) box rotini, cooked according to package directions

½ (15-ounce) can hearts of palm, drained and sliced

1 (15-ounce) can green beans, drained

1 (15-ounce) can pitted black olives, drained

1 (6-ounce) can white albacore tuna in water, drained

12 grape tomatoes, halved

2 tablespoons capers

¼ cup baby spinach leaves

For Dressing:

⅓ cup olive oil

⅓ cup mayonnaise

⅓ cup plain low-fat yogurt

2 cloves garlic, peeled

2 tablespoons fresh lemon juice

2 tablespoons fresh parsley, minced

2 tablespoons fresh dill, minced

1 teaspoon dried basil

½ teaspoon salt

Imitation bacon bits, for garnish (optional)

PREP:	8 minutes	
COOK:	9 to 11 minutes	
CHILL:	none	
YIELD:	6 servings	

○ In a salad bowl, place pasta, hearts of palm, green beans, olives, tuna, tomatoes, capers and spinach.

○ Place all dressing ingredients in blender or food processor, and mix until smooth and creamy.

○ Pour over pasta and tuna. Toss to coat evenly.

○ Garnish with imitation bacon bits, if desired.

Suggested Wine: Hagafen 2004 Reserve Estate Bottled Napa Valley Pinot Noir Fagan Creek Vineyard: Block 38. Tangy olives and smoky "bacon" bits can make for a tricky match. But this single-vineyard Pinot Noir, with its distinct spicy nature, is the perfect accompaniment.

You can add variety to this dish by adding ¼ cup anchovy fillets. Or for a sweet touch, add 2 tablespoons of Craisins. If you have loads of time, substitute fresh tuna steaks for canned tuna. Season both sides of the steaks with salt and pepper and broil or sear.

PREP: 11 minutes
COOK: 20 minutes
CHILL: none
YIELD: 8 servings

Mexican Pizzas

8   prepared individual pizza crusts

2   tablespoons olive oil

2   cups shredded cheddar cheese

2   cups shredded mozzarella cheese

1   (15-ounce) can chopped tomatoes, drained

1   (6-ounce) can tomato paste

1   (15-ounce) can kidney beans, drained

1   (15-ounce) can black beans, drained

1   (11-ounce) can sweet yellow corn Niblets, drained

½   teaspoon Tabasco sauce, or to taste

1   teaspoon salt

○ Preheat oven to 425° F. Lightly grease a cookie sheet with non-stick cooking spray.

○ Place pizza crusts on prepared cookie sheet and brush with olive oil.

○ Bake pizza crusts, uncovered, at 425° for 5 minutes.

○ Meanwhile, mix cheeses in a small bowl. Set aside.

○ In a separate bowl, combine tomatoes, tomato paste, beans, corn, Tabasco and salt.

○ Remove crusts from the oven and divide tomato mixture evenly among the 8 crusts. Spread to within about ¼-inch of edges.

○ Sprinkle with cheeses.

○ Return to oven. Bake, uncovered, at 425° for 20 minutes or until cheese is melted and pizza crusts are pale brown. Let stand 5 minutes before serving.

This delicious and nutritious Mexican-style pizza is also adapted from that fabulous handbook for good eating: *Healthy Cooking*.

Top each pizza with 2 to 3 slices of fresh avocado or a few slices of jarred hot pepper rings immediately before serving.

Parmesan and Sun-Dried Tomato-Crusted Tilapia

PREP: 11 minutes

COOK: 15 minutes

CHILL: none

YIELD: 4 servings

4   tilapia fillets, about 2½ pounds

½   teaspoon sea salt

2   tablespoons fresh dill, minced, divided

4-6 sun-dried tomatoes, chopped

¾   cup parmesan cheese

2   tablespoons olive oil

1   tablespoon lemon juice

¼   cup light mayonnaise

- Preheat oven to 450° F.

- Lightly grease a 9 x 13-inch pan with non-stick cooking spray.

- Rinse fish, pat dry and place in prepared pan.

- Sprinkle with salt and 1 tablespoon of dill.

- Bake, uncovered, at 450° for 10 minutes.

- In a bowl, mix sun-dried tomatoes, cheese, remaining dill, olive oil, lemon juice and mayonnaise.

- Remove fillets from oven and turn oven to broil; spread sun-dried tomato mixture over fish.

- Return to oven and broil for another 4 to 5 minutes, until cheese topping is slightly browned.

Suggested Wine: Hagafen 2005 Napa Valley Sauvignon Blanc. Clean-tasting tilapia needs salt and lemon juice to help bring out the creaminess of its flesh. Only Sauvignon Blanc, with its citrus components, will succeed in that context.

My friend Rozanna's mother, Lela, gave me the very simple parmesan crusted fish recipe that this dish is based on, and I thought the addition of sun-dried tomatoes was a great complement to the parmesan. If you're not a fan, leave them out. The dish will still have plenty of flavor.

Slice and sauté shallots and sprinkle them over the fish for an appealing appearance and taste.

Creamy Ziti

1   (1-pound) box ziti or penne rigate

2   (26-ounce) jars prepared marinara sauce

1   (32-ounce) container ricotta cheese

2   (8-ounce) packages shredded
    mozzarella cheese, divided

○ Preheat oven to 375° F. Lightly grease a
9 x 13-inch pan with non-stick cooking
spray.

○ Cook ziti about 2 to 3 minutes less than
package directions for al dente pasta.
Drain, rinse with cold water to stop the
cooking and set aside.

○ In a large bowl, mix marinara sauce,
ricotta and 1 cup of mozzarella.

○ Pour about 2 cups of the sauce mixture
in prepared pan, spreading over bottom.

○ Combine ziti and remaining sauce mixture
and stir until well combined, making sure
there are no dry patches of pasta. Pour
into pan and spread to edges.

○ Sprinkle remaining mozzarella over ziti
to cover.

○ Bake, covered, at 375° for 45 minutes to
1 hour. Uncover and continue baking
until cheese is golden brown and bubbly.

○ Serve hot, straight out of the pan.

Suggested Wine: Hagafen 2004 Napa Valley Zinfandel.
Zinfandel is a high-acid wine, which is the only kind of wine that will match
with tomato-based sauces.

This is it! The Geller ziti I told you
about. Hubby and I are famous in our
neighborhood for this yummy dish.
It's a quick prep, but it lasts long in
people's memories.

One of the secrets to this ziti is that
the pasta is slightly undercooked before it goes into the oven, which helps
prevent it from becoming too mushy.

Creamy Spinach Fettuccini

1 (1-pound) box spinach fettuccini

For Sauce:

1 cup chopped frozen spinach, thawed and drained

1 cup heavy cream

½ cup butter

½ cup fresh grated parmesan cheese

⅛ teaspoon onion powder

⅛ teaspoon garlic powder

1 teaspoon salt

Additional fresh grated parmesan (optional)

○ Cook fettuccini according to package directions. While pasta is cooking, prepare sauce.

○ In a 4-quart saucepan mix spinach, cream, butter, parmesan, onion and garlic powders, and salt, and simmer over low heat until combined and heated through.

○ Pour sauce over fettuccini and mix well. Serve immediately with parmesan cheese on the side, if desired.

Suggested Wine: Hagafen 2005 Napa Valley Sauvignon Blanc.

This creamy sauce calls out for contrast. Citrusy Sauvignon Blanc creates a fantastic matching of opposites that will allow each bite of the fettuccini to dance on your tongue.

If not served immediately, the sauce will dry out on the pasta. (I refuse to expose how I came across this valuable lesson. Just take my word for it.) So if not serving immediately, keep sauce and pasta separate. Reheat and mix just before serving.

Spinach and Cheddar Calzone

½ cup ricotta cheese

½ cup shredded mozzarella cheese

½ cup shredded cheddar cheese

½ cup chopped frozen spinach, thawed and drained

1 tablespoon fresh basil, minced

1 tablespoon fresh parsley, minced

1 (1-pound) raw pizza dough, from local pizza shop

1 egg

½ tablespoon sesame seeds (optional)

○ Preheat oven to 375° F. Lightly grease a cookie sheet with non-stick cooking spray.

○ In a medium bowl, mix cheeses, spinach, basil and parsley.

○ Divide dough into 4 equal parts and roll out on a floured board to about 6 inches in diameter.

○ Spoon equal amounts of filling onto each piece of pizza dough.

○ Fold over and seal edges, pinching closed with fingers or tines of a fork.

○ Place calzones on prepared cookie sheet.

○ Beat egg and brush tops of calzones. Sprinkle with sesame seeds.

○ Bake, uncovered, at 375° for 30 minutes or until dough is golden.

I adapted this recipe from *Food & Wine* magazine. When we tested this calzone, it blew us away.

Add 1 finely chopped red onion to the cheese mixture to give this dish more zip. For a yummy variation, sprinkle 1 tablespoon of cheddar cheese on top of each calzone instead of the sesame seeds.

Suggested Wine: Hagafen 2004 Oak Knoll District of Napa Valley Chardonnay. Calzones need a wine to accent their body, and this full-bodied Chardonnay will work beautifully with the cheddar and herbs in this dish.

Sole in White Wine and Butter Sauce

4   sole fillets, about 2½ pounds
⅓   cup butter, melted
½   cup seasoned bread crumbs
1   teaspoon dried parsley
3   teaspoons prepared crushed garlic

For Sauce:

¼   cup white wine
2   tablespoons lemon juice
¾   cup boiling water
1   teaspoon Osem Consommé Mix
     Lemon slices, for serving

PREP: 15 minutes
COOK: 10 minutes
CHILL: none
YIELD: 4 servings

○ Preheat oven to 425° F. Lightly grease a 9 x 13-inch pan with non-stick cooking spray.

○ Place butter in shallow bowl; place bread crumbs, parsley and garlic in another shallow bowl.

○ Rinse fish and pat dry. Dip fillets in butter, place in prepared pan and sprinkle with bread crumb mixture.

○ Bake, uncovered, at 425° for 10 minutes.

○ Meanwhile, for sauce, pour wine into a saucepan and cook for 3 to 5 minutes over medium heat, stirring occasionally.

○ Mix in lemon juice, water and consommé mix. Bring to a boil over medium-high heat, and continue boiling until sauce reduces by about half and thickens.

○ Place fish on a platter or individual plates. Spoon sauce over fillets and garnish with lemon.

Suggested Wine: Hagafen 2004 Oak Knoll District of Napa Valley Chardonnay. This Chardonnay has a little bit of creaminess to it, which will complement the buerre blanc sauce of this dish. For added matching, use the wine in the recipe.

There is nothing quite like Dover sole, and this recipe was initially created for that fish. It is quite expensive and hard to come by, so flounder or other kinds of sole (grey or lemon sole) are a great substitute. Salmon would work here, too.

PREP: 10 minutes

COOK: 40 to 50 minutes

CHILL: none

YIELD: 4 to 6 servings

Linguini and Tomato
Sauce Florentine

1   (1-pound) box linguini

For Sauce:

1   tablespoon olive oil

2   tablespoons prepared crushed garlic

1   small onion, diced

1   (24-ounce) can tomato sauce

1   (16-ounce) package chopped frozen
    spinach, thawed and drained

$\frac{1}{3}$ cup grated parmesan cheese

3   tablespoons heavy cream

1   teaspoon salt

$\frac{1}{4}$ teaspoon coarse black pepper

○ Cook linguini according to package directions. While pasta is cooking, prepare
   sauce.

○ In a 10-inch skillet, heat olive oil over
   medium heat.

○ Add garlic, sauté for 1 minute. Add onion
   and sauté until soft and lightly golden.

○ Add tomato sauce, spinach and cheese,
   stirring well.

○ Add cream, salt and pepper, and stir.

○ Reduce heat and simmer, covered, for
   30 minutes. Pour over pasta and toss.

This recipe is an Aunt Rachel original.
It has the aroma and sophisticated
taste of a complex Italian dish, without a day's worth of work.

This sauce is also delish over grilled
fish such as tuna, sea bass or halibut.

Blintz Soufflé

PREP: 7 minutes

COOK: 45 minutes

CHILL: none

YIELD: 6 to 8 servings

315

10-12 frozen blintzes, assorted flavors,
       defrosted just enough to separate

1   cup sour cream

¼   cup sugar

¼   cup orange juice

4   eggs, beaten

2   tablespoons butter, melted

2   teaspoons pure vanilla extract

⅛   teaspoon salt

1   tablespoon cinnamon sugar

       Additional sour cream, for serving
       (optional)

○ Preheat oven to 350° F.

○ Place blintzes in a 9 x 13-inch pan.

○ In a medium bowl, mix together sour cream,
  sugar, orange juice, eggs, butter, vanilla
  and salt. Pour mixture over blintzes.

○ Sprinkle with cinnamon sugar.

○ Bake, uncovered, at 350° for 45 minutes,
  until puffed and golden. Serve with sour
  cream on the side, if desired.

I never met a soufflé that I didn't like,
and they like me, too. They tend to
settle contentedly on my hips. Blintzes
are classic in the Jewish cooking world
and every chef has his or her own version of this soufflé. You really can't go
wrong with all that butter, cream,
sugar and eggs.

If you have an attractive baking dish,
use it. This is a soufflé best served
right out of the dish at the table.

Berry Brulée

PREP: 7 minutes

COOK: 2 to 4 minutes

CHILL: none

YIELD: 4 servings

2   cups assorted frozen berries such as strawberries, raspberries and blueberries

4   teaspoons fruit liqueur

½   cup heavy cream

1   cup prepared vanilla custard or pudding

½   cup turbinado sugar (Sugar in the Raw)

○ Preheat broiler.

○ Divide berries evenly among four 7-ounce ramekins.

○ In a small bowl mix together liqueur, heavy cream and custard, and spoon over berries.

○ Sprinkle 2 tablespoons sugar over each serving.

○ Broil 2 to 4 minutes until sugar melts and caramelizes, turning brown and bubbly. Serve while still hot.

Another delicious *Healthy Cooking* adaptation, the original recipe calls for fresh berries, which take more time. Along with the fruit liquor, the frozen berries emit a juice that you will want to slurp up with a straw, almost like a soup. Half the fun is breaking into the caramelized topping for your berry surprise.

Since you need only 4 teaspoons of liqueur, just buy one of those cute little airline-sized bottles.

Suggested Wine: Hagafen 2001 Napa Valley Brut Cuvée Sparkling Wine. The white chocolate and berries in the Brut Cuvée are a superb match for the berries and caramelized vanilla, making this a classy yet simple dessert pairing.

Sufganiot (Jelly Doughnuts)

PREP: 8 minutes

COOK: 10 minutes

REST: 20 minutes

YIELD: 14 doughnuts

2½ cups self-rising flour

2 (8-ounce) cartons vanilla low-fat yogurt

2 tablespoons vanilla sugar

2 eggs

6 cups canola oil

¾ cup confectioners' sugar

1 cup seedless strawberry jelly

○ In a large bowl, place flour, yogurt, vanilla sugar and eggs.

○ Knead until all ingredients are combined and a sticky, doughy batter is formed. Cover with a kitchen towel and let it rest for 15 to 20 minutes.

○ Heat 6 cups canola oil in a 6-quart stockpot, covered, over medium heat.

○ When dough is ready, uncover oil and raise heat to high.

○ Scoop out a tablespoonful of batter and drop in oil. Don't make the doughnuts too big, so they can cook through.

○ You should be able to fry about 7 doughnuts at a time. Using a slotted spoon, turn doughnuts when halfway browned, about 30 seconds to 1 minute. Fry for another 2 to 3 minutes or until entire doughnut is deep golden brown and cooked through.

○ Remove doughnuts and let cool on paper towel-lined plates. Repeat previous 2 steps with remaining batter.

○ Fill a squeeze bottle with jelly and inject a little into each doughnut.

○ Roll each doughnut in confectioners' sugar. Or, shake 3 doughnuts at a time in a paper bag filled with confectioners' sugar.

319

My sister-in-law Carly and I attempted this recipe one Chanukah night when the whole family came over for candle-lighting. Everyone got involved. Some of us were on deep-fry duty, some of us powdered and the rest "quality control" tasted. We all had a blast. There was flour and confectioners' sugar everywhere.

PREP: 6 minutes

COOK: none

CHILL: 8 hours or overnight,
plus 1 hour in refrigerator

YIELD: 8 servings

Peanut Butter Ice Cream Pie

1   pint vanilla ice cream, slightly thawed, divided

1   (9-inch) prepared graham cracker piecrust

¾   cup smooth peanut butter

½   cup chocolate chips

¾   cup peanut butter chips, divided

○ Spread half of the ice cream in graham cracker piecrust.

○ Dot peanut butter all over ice cream.

○ Sprinkle with chocolate chips and ½ cup of peanut butter chips, dispersing evenly.

○ Spread remaining ice cream over top.

○ Cover top with remaining peanut butter chips.

○ Freeze overnight, or at least 8 hours.

○ Soften for 1 hour in refrigerator before serving to make it easier to cut and so the chips will not be too hard to bite into.

I had kids in mind when I came up with this dessert, but as with many things targeted to little ones, grown-ups wound up loving it, too. I found myself watching that the kids only had one slice because I didn't want their bellies to hurt. Then, I'd sneak a second slice for myself when they weren't looking. Hey, I have a bigger mouth; I need more ice cream, right?

A combination of chocolate and vanilla ice cream makes a "black-and-white" ice cream pie.

Shortbread

3   cups flour

½   cup sugar

½   cup light brown sugar, packed

1   egg

2   sticks butter

○ Preheat oven to 325° F.

○ Mix all ingredients in food processor until combined, about 3 to 4 minutes.

○ Press dough into an 8-inch square baking pan and pierce all over with tines of a fork. Score dough into squares.

○ Bake at 325° for 1 hour. Let cool, and store in an airtight container. Before serving, cut into squares.

Adapted from a recipe in *The Mothers' Center Cookbook*, this is moist and crispy at the same time! Is such a thing possible? I think of it as sort of a cookie cake, with the best attributes of both. True shortbread is made without eggs. So this recipe is not traditional, but it's still delicious, so I don't care. Do you?

Shortbread originated in Scotland, where it is still considered something of a national food. Old-fashioned cooks spoke of a baked dessert made with plenty of shortening as being "short."

PREP: 9 minutes

COOK: 45 minutes

CHILL: none

YIELD: 8 servings

Strawberry Cream
Cheese Roll

1   frozen puff pastry sheet (from a
     17.3-ounce package), defrosted

½   cup cream cheese

¼   cup ricotta cheese

1   cup strawberry pie filling

1   egg

2   tablespoons confectioners sugar
     (optional)

○ Preheat oven to 350° F. Lightly grease a
  cookie sheet with non-stick baking spray.

○ Unfold pastry sheet on a flat work surface.

○ In a small bowl, mix cream cheese, ricotta
  and strawberry filling.

○ Place cream cheese mixture on about ⅓
  of pastry dough and roll as for a jelly roll.

○ Place roll, seam side down, on prepared
  cookie sheet.

○ Beat egg and brush the outside of roll.

○ Bake, uncovered, at 350° for 45 minutes,
  until puffed up and golden.

○ Dust with confectioners sugar if desired
  and slice into 8 pieces. Serve warm or at
  room temperature.

Suggested Wine: Hagafen 2005 Potter Valley White Riesling.
Delicate fruits likes strawberries need a wine that won't overwhelm them.
This Riesling has enough residual sugar to be sweet, but not so much as
to overshadow the dessert.

When my recipe tester, Joy, served
these to a group of friends, they were
dying to know how we got the filling
to be that pretty pink color. There was
such intrigue and we held back, not
divulging any of our quickie cookbook
secrets. But now it can be revealed!
Ta-da!

Serve on individual plates and garnish
with a sliced fanned strawberry and
some strawberry sauce for decoration.
You might also sprinkle with sliced
almonds.

Chocolate Chip
Cheesecake

PREP: 7 minutes
COOK: 40 to 50 minutes
CHILL: 4 hours
YIELD: 6 to 8 servings

1½ (8-ounce) packages cream cheese, softened

¼   cup sugar

¼   cup light brown sugar, packed

2   eggs

1   teaspoon pure vanilla extract

1   cup chocolate chips

1   (9-inch) prepared chocolate or plain graham cracker crust

½   cup pie filling or ½ cup sour cream (optional)

○ Preheat oven to 350° F.

○ Using an electric mixer at medium speed, mix cream cheese and sugars together until smooth. Add eggs, one at a time, mixing into batter. When fully blended, mix in vanilla.

○ Using a silicone spatula, fold in chocolate chips.

○ Pour into graham cracker crust.

○ Bake at 350° for 40 to 50 minutes or until just slightly jiggly in the center. The cake will finish cooking from the retained heat after you take it out of the oven.

○ Chill in refrigerator for at least 4 hours before serving.

○ Before serving top with either a layer of sour cream or your favorite flavor pie filling, if desired.

Suggested Wine: Hagafen 2005 Napa Valley Late Harvest Zinfandel. Chocolate demands late-harvest Zinfandel. The oak and fruit, plus the residual sugar, will make the chocolate more intense.

If you want to transform this into a chocolate swirl cheesecake, squirt chocolate syrup on top and use a knife to create a zigzag swirl design before putting it in the oven. Not big on chocolate? Just omit the chips and it's a classic cheesecake.

Jewish Holidays and the Family Chef

When I was just starting out on my Jewish journey, I was invited to many homes to share a Shabbos meal with my knowledgeable hosts. Sure, I loved going to those big, warm, delicious, filled-with-love Shabbos dinners every week. But cooking them? I didn't even know how to make toast. (Mom taught me how to accessorize.) Once I was married, I was determined to replicate those wonderful meals and invite the whole world, or at least a couple dozen extended family members. To say the least, I had a lot to learn.

First of all, there's the question of quantity. A lot of people I know invite eight or 10 guests for Thanksgiving. It's their big, once-a-year bash. So let me put it this way: Shabbos meals are like two Thanksgiving meals every weekend, and holidays (some of which are a week long) are four to six Thanksgiving meals, back to back.

We're talking the works here, people. That phrase about "everything but the kitchen sink" must have been invented to describe Jewish eating. The typical Shabbos meal often consists of fresh-baked challah; one or two apps (fish, usually); soup; at least one or two mains (chicken and meat); a kugel or two; salads (yes, plural); and several dessert options.

Don't panic! I'm here to help you. You're not obligated to feed your family, a traveling circus troupe, seven exchange students and those new people from down the block – at least not right away. And you don't have to go overboard and offer "everything *and* the kitchen sink," as you'll see when you get to my suggested menus. Even if you're a diffident cook, you'll soon find yourself becoming more and more daring. Before long, you'll be putting as many people as you can fit around your table, adding a table, borrowing more tables and chairs, just so you can enjoy more guests. It's *heimishe*. What does that mean? Well, it's Yiddish for homey and warm. We prepare a formal meal and then take the stuffiness right out of it. That's what Shabbos and our holidays are all about.

I've made it as easy for you as I can. Here are menu plans, complete with

wine suggestions for every course, because sometimes it's
hard to mix and match recipes and figure out what goes
well together and what wines pair nicely with your choices.
The menus reflect the tone of the holiday as well as the
food customs associated with it. So, I did the hard work
for you – including taste-testing all the recipes! A painstaking task, but somebody had to do it.

The holidays are a great time to try out special recipes
and even make up new ones. As my grandmother would
say, eat and enjoy!

Holiday Menus:
It's Tradition!
A quickie intro to Jewish festivals and feasting

Jews are called the "People of the Book." I think we got this rep because we're always booking friends and relatives to attend our numerous feasts. "Oh, it'll be just a small gathering; maybe 15 or 20 of us for a nice little Shabbos lunch."

Just about all of our holidays are of biblical origin, so you can bet we've been doing them for centuries and we've got them down pat.

As I was learning about Judaism, I discovered holidays they never taught us about in school. You may be familiar with some or all of them. I sure wasn't. I've come to love every single one, because each represents a special event in the history of the Jewish people.

So here it is: the Jewish calendar according to Jamie. I've provided one menu per holiday, but you'll find lots of creative ideas for other meals among the recipes in this book.

The photograph on the left was taken in 1964 at the Jewish Community Center in Genova, Italy. The children, shown participating in a Purim party, are emigrants from Romania, Hungary and Czechoslovakia. They, along with their families, are waiting in Genova for entry visas into the United States.

That's my uncle Mike at 7 years old, front and center, a bespectacled King Achashvarosh. And that's my mom, at 12, standing in the back row just to the left of the Jewish star. She has short black hair and is dressed as the most famous Purim player, Queen Esther. My family was celebrating a very special Purim en route from Transylvania, Romania, to Philadelphia, Pennsylvania. This incredible image captures their excitement and hope as they dream of their new life in America.

Shabbos

Chief among our traditional banquets are the weekly Shabbos meals. (Sabbath can be pronounced in Hebrew either as Shabbat or Shabbos. Take your pick.) Shabbos attests to the creation of the world by G-d and is one of the hallmarks of observant Judaism. This concept gives rise to the laws of Shabbos, some prohibiting various mundane activities, others obligating us to make the day special by doing certain things – such as saying Kiddush (a prayer over wine) and inviting everyone you've ever met over for a meal. The majority of these rules apply to the holidays as well. The most significant difference – at least to the female half of the population – is that we don't cook on Shabbos (though we have tricks to keep our food hot!), but we are permitted to cook on the holidays.

Traditional Shabbos foods include gefilte fish, chicken soup and kugel. Potato kugel is standard, but my challah kugel is another take on it.

Shabbos Dinner

Challah	Pull-Apart Challah *(p. 245)*
Appetizer	Chilled Salmon with Dijon Dipping Sauce *(p. 37)*
Soup	Classic Chicken Soup *(p. 63)*
Entrée	Roasted Garlic Chicken and Baby Vegetables *(p. 127)*
	Mushroom and Wine Silvertip Roast *(p. 157)*
Side	Challah Kugel *(p. 189)*
	Baby French String Beans with Slivered Almonds *(p. 183)*
Dessert	One Bowl Amazing Chocolate Cake *(p. 231)*
Wine	Hagafen 2003 Estate Bottled Napa Valley Merlot

Rosh Hashanah

This is the birthday of mankind. Though it's a holiday that is joyous, it's also sobering because it's the time when the fates of nations and individuals for the coming year are ordained. To symbolize our wishes for a "sweet" year, our meals emphasize foods that are sweet. Tart or bitter foods are a no-no.

At our Rosh Hashanah table, round challahs are used to symbolize the yearly cycle of life. In this menu, Honey Chicken and Cran-Apple Crunch Kugel echo our tradition of eating apples and honey. Teriyaki Skirt Steak is also a sweet little dish.

Rosh Hashanah Dinner

Challah	Round Cinnamon Raisin Challah *(p. 245)*
Salad	Warm Salmon Salad *(p. 77)*
Entrée	Honey Chicken *(p. 138)*
	Teriyaki Skirt Steak *(p. 156)*
Side	Cran-Apple Crunch Kugel *(p. 205)*
	Baked Spicy Sweet Potato Fries *(p. 181)*
Dessert	Peanut Butter Chocolate Chip Mousse Pie *(p. 236)*
Wine	Hagafen 2001 Estate Bottled Napa Valley Syrah

The most somber day of the year, it's also called the Day of Atonement. It reminds us that we are all accountable for our actions. The concept of "New Year's resolutions" that mark our secular New Year's Day comes from the Jewish idea of repentance at the start of a new year. As we reflect on the mistakes we've made over the past year, we resolve to be better people. One element of repentance is fasting, so Jews are not permitted to eat or drink on Yom Kippur. But boy, do we prepare ourselves for the fast! We serve full, balanced meals – light on the salt and thirst-inducing spices – just before the fast. When it's over, we give thanks and dig in once again.

Round challah is used throughout the high holidays and Sukkos. At the pre-Yom Kippur meal we want to eat well, but not overstuff ourselves. So I've kept the menu light with a vegetable soup and delicate Cornish hens. Potatoes and rice salad are important, as carbs sustain us through the fast. Dessert is a cool, sorbet treat – refreshing, but not rich or heavy.

Pre-Yom Kippur Menu

Challah	Round Sesame and Poppy Seed Challah *(p. 245)*
Soup	Purée of Bean and Vegetable Soup *(p. 51)*
Entrée	Roasted Cornish Hens with Fingerling Roasted Potatoes *(p. 135)*
Side	Broccoli Kugel *(p. 188)*
Salad	Long Grain and Wild Rice Salad *(p. 83)*
Dessert	Tea Biscuit and Sorbet Tower *(p. 213)*

Sukkos

This is the time of year when we build a sukkah, a temporary structure roofed by branches or bamboo. It commemorates the flimsy desert huts the Israelites lived in for 40 years after the Exodus from Egypt. Although it's supposed to serve as living quarters, the sukkah is far from secure. The idea is that it represents our trust in G-d, rather than material shelters, to protect us. The obligation is to eat our meals and even sleep in the sukkah.

The beef porridge on this menu is a thick and filling soup, perfect for warming up your guests in the sukkah, especially in colder regions. As Sukkos is a time for inviting lots of guests (and there are always drop-ins as well!) turkey is the greatest main dish. There's always enough! Cranberry relish complements it superbly. The Pumpkin Pie recipe serves 16 – a big crowd pleaser, literally!

Sukkos Menu

Challah	Round Maple Syrup and Craisin Challah *(p. 245)*
Appetizer	Spiced Gefilte Fish *(p. 33)*
Soup	Beef Porridge *(p. 55)*
Entrée	Roasted Turkey *(p. 143)*
	Stuffed Peppers *(p. 151)*
Side	Cranberry Relish *(p. 185)*
	Roasted Sweet Vegetables in Spicy Cinnamon Cider *(p. 199)*
Dessert	Pumpkin Pie *(p. 226)*
Wine	Hagafen 2002 Estate Bottled Napa Valley Cabernet Sauvignon

Shemini Atzeres is the day after Sukkos, but it's a separate holiday. It's regarded as a time to celebrate the special relationship between G-d and the Jewish people, sort of an intimate gathering of several million people with their Creator.

Simchas Torah celebrates the privilege of studying the Torah, a unique aspect of Jewish life and survival. It's the holiday when the Torah scrolls are taken out of the ark and carried around the synagogue, amidst wild singing and dancing. Little kids wave flags and the whole atmosphere is charged with super-duper joy. Of course you know what all this hoopla means to the Jewish homemaker: Bring on the food!

Torah scrolls are rolled on wooden spindles, so I chose rolled foods for our menu: a deli roll and pinwheel cookies. The wine ingredients add to the festivity of the occasion, too.

Shemini Atzeres-Simchas Torah Menu

Challah	Round Chocolate Chip Challah *(p. 245)*
Appetizer	Deli Roll *(p. 29)*
Entrée	Brisket in Wine Sauce *(p. 152)*
Side	Broccolini in a Creamy Wine Balsamic Sauce *(p. 195)*
	Herb Roasted Red Bliss Potatoes *(p. 197)*
Dessert	Raspberry Twists *(p. 211)*
	Pinwheels *(p. 212)*
Wine	Hagafen 2001 Estate Bottled Napa Valley Syrah

Chanukah

Ironically, Chanukah, the most widely known Jewish holiday among non-Jews, celebrates the distinction of the Jewish people from other groups. When the land of Israel was occupied by Syrian rulers who outlawed the practicing of Judaism, a minority of pious Jews opted to fight for their religion rather than give in to assimilation. Miraculously, they were able to drive off the enemy.

So where does the oil come in? When the Jewish army wanted to rededicate the desecrated Holy Temple, they needed pure oil to light its golden menorah. The small amount found was enough to last for just one day, but it lasted for eight. This miracle demonstrated that the Jewish victory was thanks to G-d's direct intervention. The holiday of Chanukah was declared – along with the custom of eating yummy treats fried in oil.

Chanukah Menu

Challah	Challah Garlic Bread *(p. 247)*
Appetizer	Mozzarella and Tomato Stacks *(p. 283)*
Entrée	Parmesan and Sun-dried Tomato Crusted Tilapia *(p. 305)*
	Creamy Ziti *(p. 307)*
Side	Latkes *(p. 192)*
Salad	Sun-dried Tomato Caesar Salad *(p. 73)*
Dessert	Sufganiot *(p. 319)*
Wine	Hagafen 2005 Napa Valley Sauvignon Blanc

Purim

Read through *Megillas Esther* (The Book of Esther), and you'll understand instantly why this is a holiday. While the Jews were threatened spiritually on their home turf at the time of the Chanukah miracles, the Jews of Persia were threatened physically on Purim. A series of wild "coincidences" saved them, events so unbelievable that Queen Esther and Morde-chai (her uncle, who happened to be the leading sage at the time) saw the hand of G-d in them every step of the way. The holiday of Purim, with its masks and costumes alluding to the hidden, mysterious workings behind the scenes, was the result. A favorite treat on Purim is hamantashen, a triangular pastry containing a hidden filling!

In place of hamantashen, Chocolate Liqueur Pie concludes this meal of hearty dishes, adding to the celebratory mood. I think of this as a meal men will appreciate – even if they become a little light-headed, if you get my drift.

Purim Menu

Challah	Poppy and Sesame Seed Challah *(p. 245)*
Appetizer	Stuffed Mushrooms *(p. 26)*
Entrée	Asian Steak *(p. 161)*
Side	Broccoli and Mushroom Pie *(p. 193)*
	Baked Spicy Sweet Potato Fries *(p. 181)*
Dessert	Chocolate Liqueur Pie *(p. 233)*
Wine	Hagafen 2001 Estate Bottled Napa Valley Syrah

Passover

The biggie. Pesach.

There's probably no holiday on the Jewish calendar – no holiday on anybody's calendar – that has as much to do with food as Passover. Kosher for Passover fare contains no leavening, but observance goes beyond chucking the bread out and bringing in the matzoh for a week. It involves different sets of cookware, dishes, recipes and a different mindset altogether. It's the holiday our grandmothers dubbed "a kitchen yuntif" because we spend so much time preparing meals. And though I'm committed to fast and easy recipes year-round, there's something about Passover that makes me enjoy every minute I spend in the kitchen, making this holiday even more memorable for my family. Call me crazy.

The Passover seder menu is not a super-duper, multi-course affair because the seder service mandates consuming a good deal of matzoh and wine prior to the meal itself. In fact, over the course of the seder, four cups of wine are consumed, so it's important to choose a wine that is not too intoxicating and will not feel heavy on the stomach. In many homes, the seder meal itself isn't served until quite late at night – all the more reason to keep the meal and the seder wine light.

Passover Seder Menu

Soup	Un-Stuffed Cabbage Soup *(p. 59)*
Entrée	Speedy Coq Au Vin *(p. 131)*
Side	Potato Kugel Cups *(p. 191)*
	Italian Zucchini *(p. 180)*
Salad	Baby Spinach and Portobello Mushroom Salad *(p. 75)*
Dessert	Chocolate-Covered Matzohs *(p. 239)*
	"Forgotten" Macaroons *(p.227)*
Wine	Hagafen 2003 Estate Bottled Napa Valley Merlot or
	Hagafen 2000 Estate Bottled Napa Valley Syrah

On the following page you'll find a full list of all the recipes that can be adapted for Pesach, complete with notes regarding minor adjustments when necessary.

Just a note about "Kosher for Passover" products: Many supermarkets and groceries offer a wide variety of foods and ingredients that are permissible for Passover use. Remember that all ingredients and products (including ketchup, mayonnaise, soda and processed foods) must be certified kosher for Passover. A Passover guide published annually by the Orthodox Union, the OU kashrus supervising agency, is comprehensive and lists products that are certified kosher for Passover as well as products that do not need special Passover supervision. The guide is available about one month before Passover. You can download it for free online at www.oukosher.org. You can find a print version in many stores or you can order it from the Orthodox Union directly at 11 Broadway, 14th Floor, New York, NY, 10004.

The recipes on this menu and in the chart that follows are easily adaptable to Passover, as long as you get your ingredients with reliable kosher for Passover certifications when necessary. Refer to the Adjustment column for specific items that should be omitted entirely because they are either not kosher for Passover or not available with kosher for Passover certification. The Adjustment column also includes substitutions where applicable. And be sure to consult with a rabbi when it comes to preparing your kitchen, (oven, microwave, countertops) and your house in general for Passover.

RECIPE	PAGE	ADJUSTMENT
Appetizers		
Classic Gefilte Fish	31	
Cold Smoked Fish Salad	35	Omit the flatbreads or rye
Sweet and Sour Salmon	34	Omit the crushed red pepper flakes
Soups		
Mango Strawberry Soup	65	
Un-Stuffed Cabbage Soup	59	
Classic Chicken Soup	63	
Salads		
Italian Tomato Salad	87	Substitute fresh, frozen or dried garlic powder for prepared crushed garlic
Israeli Salad	93	
Israeli Cabbage Salad	86	
Baby Spinach and Portobello Mushroom Salad	74	Substitute fresh, frozen or dried garlic powder for prepared crushed garlic
Sweet Carrot Salad	79	Substitute extra light olive oil for canola oil
Fish		
Crispy Rainbow Trout	111	
Cod in a Light Lime Sauce	115	Omit the brown rice
Poultry		
Baked Oniony Chicken	129	
Speedy Coq Au Vin	131	

Shavuos

Okay, another holiday that's relatively obscure outside the shtetl. But it shouldn't be. It's actually one of the basic celebrations of Judaism. It comes seven weeks after Passover and is actually the culmination of that famous festival. The Jews got out of Egypt on Passover, but the goal was not simply freedom from slavery. The object was to galvanize them into a nation committed to teaching the world that there's a G-d. They were to live life on a higher plane, becoming a nation that would serve as the model of a perfect society. The means to reaching that ideal is the Torah, which the Jews received at the foot of Mount Sinai on Shavuos.

Now that's certainly one of the most historic events ever, but because there are no specific observances attached – no seder or Chanukah candles – Shavuos is all but forgotten, except among Torah-observant Jews. It's a beautiful holiday, full of interesting customs, many of which revolve around – you guessed it – food. Dairy meals are *de rigueur* on Shavuos, because that's what the Jews ate at Sinai when they realized they didn't know how to prepare kosher meat!

This beautiful menu features dairy food in keeping with tradition. I'm not sure when cheesecake became associated with this holiday, but I'm glad it did!

Shavuos Menu

Soup	French Onion Soup *(p. 281)*
Entrée	Sole in White Wine and Butter Sauce *(p. 312)* Blintz Soufflé *(p. 315)*
Side	Cheese Quiche *(p. 295)*
Salad	Goat Cheese Walnut Salad *(p. 299)*
Dessert	Chocolate Chip Cheesecake *(p. 325)*
Wine	Hagafen 2004 Oak Knoll District of Napa Valley Chardonnay

Why There's Yiddish in This Book

Yiddish is an amazing language. It can capture an entire idea in a single word. In my family, we speak several languages, but none have a turn of phrase as witty and dead-on as Yiddish. The downside of this is that Yiddish is practically impossible to translate.

The sound of the language expresses the feeling of each word beyond its definition.

Take *shmata*, for instance. Literally it means "rag," but it could imply a really worn-out, dirty, used-up, washed-out old thing. If you say, "I feel like a *shmata*," nothing else needs to be said! Now I just said it *could* imply that, because it could also simply mean an article of clothing. Picture the scenario: Growing up I would drag my father shopping for yet another skirt, and he would exclaim, "What do you need another *shmata* for? Your closet is full of them!" That's what's so delicious about Yiddish – your tone is all-important. Most Yiddish words have multiple definitions, yet somehow you always know what they mean.

They say Yiddish is a dying language because it's native to Eastern European Jews, immigrants to this country who are of my grandparents' generation. I beg to differ with this popular notion. In Chassidic circles all over the world, Yiddish is in the best of health. You can stand in the streets of these burgeoning enclaves and hear little children playing in Yiddish, with their mothers calling to them in this lively language. And in numerous yeshivas, both Chassidic and non-Chassidic, the language of Talmud instruction is Yiddish.

Many Yiddish terms have also found their way into English dictionaries and American parlance. I know of an English professor (who is not Jewish) who spoke to his class for 15 minutes on how some individual words capture an essence of meaning like no other. "Do you want to know my favorite word in the English language?" he asked. Then, after a dramatic pause, he said, "It's chutzpah!"

This glossary of Yiddish, Hebrew and Arabic terms used in my book will be helpful to anyone unfamiliar with these languages. If you do happen to know them, I apologize in advance. I realize it's impossible to accurately translate *mama loshen*, but at least I tried.

GLOSSARY

Baalas Teshuvah (Hebrew)

One who was not raised Orthodox, but who explored Jewish religion and culture, and as a result took on religious observance. This is the feminine construction of the term. A male would be referred to as a *baal teshuvah*. There are so many people who are *BT*'s today that it has become a vibrant sub-culture of Orthodoxy.

Balabusta (Yiddish)

The perfect homemaker. She cooks, she cleans, she bakes, she owns the best spice rack. And she does it all with grace, donating her spare time to local charities. To show you how low the bar was for me, when I successfully microwaved dinner without setting off the smoke alarm, my dad proudly called me "a real *balabusta!*"

Blech (Yiddish)

Not a term of disgust, though it sounds like one! It's just a metal stove-top cover used on Shabbos to keep cooked foods warm.

Bubby (Yiddish)

Nanny, Grammy, Grandma – the woman with the soft wrinkles and soft arms, candy in her pocket and a tissue up her sleeve, hugging you and telling you it will all be okay. A bubby's chicken soup has serious healing powers.

Challah (Hebrew)

Perhaps the most delicious bread in the world. It's almost a cake, and has the calories to prove it. It's the traditional bread of Shabbos and Jewish holidays. Yes, it can put 10 pounds on you in a flash – but it's so good, who cares?

Chulent (Yiddish)

The slowest cooking beef and bean stew in existence. You start it before Shabbos and it simmers all night until it's served the next day. Its rich aroma fills the house. The Yiddish term comes from the French word for warm, *chaud*, as chulent was developed as a means of putting piping hot food on the table in honor of Shabbos. In non-Yiddish-speaking countries, Sephardic Jews call this dish *chamin*, which means the same thing.

Chutzpah (Yiddish)

Unbelievable gall. The classic example is the man who murders both his parents and then pleads for mercy from the court – because he's an orphan!

Fancy Schmancy (English-Yiddish)

Posh; Upper East Side; absurdly elegant. Anything can be fancy schmancy: your outfit, your mansion, your nails, your poodle.

Hummus (Arabic)

Only the best Middle Eastern chickpea dip ever. But you obviously see why we need an exotic name for it. Who would try it if it were just called "chickpea dip"?

Kugel (Yiddish)

The essential Jewish carb. More like an English pudding than anything else, it can fill you for three days. It's a Shabbos classic, so some people have an insatiable addiction to it. It used to be made of either potatoes or noodles, but now it has developed into a score of varieties, from apple kugel and pineapple kugel to vegetable kugel, to you-name-it kugel.

Latkes (Yiddish)

Potato pancakes fried in oil, customary on Chanukah, but so good you may add them to your repertoire year-round. The oil is a reminder of the rededication of the Temple in Jerusalem, when a small jar of oil meant to last for one day miraculously lasted for eight. But I bet these won't last more than eight minutes. They're usually eaten straight from the pan, with family and guests standing over you as you fry. You're lucky if you get them to the table.

Mama Loshen (Yiddish)
"Mother tongue", i.e. Yiddish, but somehow the term seems a lot warmer in the original. It reminds you of lullabies, fresh butter and big family gatherings.

Mazel (Hebrew)
[Good] Fortune, a little helping hand from the One above. A mazel is not always good, but no one ever talks about bad mazel. At worst, one has "no mazel."

Potchke (Yiddish)
Fuss. As in, "I never thought I would want to potchke in the kitchen." It's one of those interesting words that's both a verb and a noun, as in "I wouldn't try cooking that; it's such a potchke."

Sephardic Jews (Hebrew)
Jews whose ancestry hails from countries south of Spain. (The Hebrew word "Sepharad" means "Spain.") They could be from Syria, Portugal, Turkey, Iran, Morocco, Israel. Definitely not from Philadelphia. Jews from Eastern Europe are referred to as Ashkenazic.

Shabbos (Hebrew)
The day to disconnect from your workday chores, worries and mundane activities. It's the day to recharge spiritual batteries through praying, studying Torah, napping and, of course, eating well. A great family experience.

Shtick (Yiddish)
(As in "not my shtick") So not my thing; not my style.

Shtetl (Yiddish)
A really small village in Eastern Europe. If you blink when you ride through it, you'll miss it. Since most *shtetlach* were destroyed during the Holocaust, the word has come to mean any Jewish enclave where religious Jews go about their lives. It's a warm, homey place, where everybody knows everybody's shtick. (See above.) Definitely not Philadelphia.

Shul (Yiddish)
Synagogue. Somehow the Yiddish term is far more popular, maybe because "synagogue" sounds so very Latin. Shul actually means "school" in Yiddish and German, and evokes the use of the shul as a place to gather and to learn Torah at all hours of the day and night, as well as a place where religious services are held.

Sufganiot (Hebrew)
Fried, powdered and jelly-filled doughnuts typically eaten on Chanukah or at your local kosher Dunkin' Donuts year-round.

Tahini (Arabic)
Middle Eastern sesame paste dip. Like hummus, it's a standard Israeli dip, one that Americans have come to know and love (but can never quite replicate, unless they follow the instructions in this book).

Tchotchkes (Yiddish)
Knickknacks, the stuff your husband or wife has covering every bit of counter space, so there's nowhere to set down the mail or your keys.

Yeshivas (Hebrew)
Plural of yeshiva, a school dedicated to teaching Jewish religion, culture and pride to the next generation of Jews. It's the place most *BT*'s didn't go as children, and wish they had.

Yom Tov (Hebrew)
Literally a "Good Day," a generic term for Jewish holidays. It's a time to pull out all the stops when it comes to your menu.

Yuntif (Yiddishization of Yom Tov)
It's a form of Old World slang used even by people whose only Yiddish consists of naming the parts of a chicken. They will greet each other in the street (whether or not they're actually acquainted) during a Jewish festival with a smile and a nod and a "Goot Yuntif!"

Many Thanks:
Many thanks to those who helped me in so many ways

MANY THANKS TO THOSE WHO
HELPED ME IN SO MANY WAYS.

I want to express my gratitude to
HaKadosh Baruch Hu for giving
me this and every opportunity, for
all the blessings He has bestowed
upon me, for my life, for my family
and for this book.

First came the idea ...
Nachum, there are no words. Suffice to say
thank you for letting me share our lives with
the readers of this book – who will forever
think of you as Hubby! Baby Bracha Miriam,
you are a bracha, a true precious gift from
Hashem. I never experienced the power of a
mother's love until I had you. Baby Rochel
Naami, we wrote this book together. While
I pounded away at the keyboard, you were
growing and learning Torah. As our family
grew with you, so did my heart, in ways I
never imagined.

Then came the proposal ...
Jon, a super talented writer, the proposal we
wrote became the blueprint for this book.
Rozanna, you edited my proposal, my résumé,
my pitch letters – my life! You have always
been there for me, delighting me with your
skills, smarts and expansive heart.

Then came the publishers: the Feldheim
team ...
Yitzchak, I am ever grateful for the opportunity. And thank you for all the brachos along
the way. I know Hashem hears you. Mendy, a
big dreamer and a big believer in me. Thanks
for bringing another cookbook into the fold.

Eli Meir, your hard work and belief in this book are the foundation of
its successful publication.

Then came the recipes ...
Thank you to all the people who gave of their time and recipe boxes
and were inspirations for many of the delicious dishes in this book. I
will never forget you and my bathroom scale will never forgive you.
Abbie, Abby, Adam, Anita, Basha, Beth, Chanie, Dani, Debbie, Devo-
rah, Donna, Geanie, Goldie, Grandma Martha, Jennie, Joan, Judi, Judy,
Karen, Lauren G., Lauren L., Lila, Magdi, Michelle, Mom, Monet, Morse,
Nachum, Rachel, Rebbetzin Heller, Rozanna, Sarah, Sylvia, Tamar,
Tamara and Uputzi.

Then came the recipe testing ...
Tzipora, just when I thought no one could help me, you recommended
Joy – that sweet and savvy recipe tester down the block. Joy Lynn and
family: Dovid, Aliza, Yitzi, Hilly, Kasriel, Meira, Adina, no one can believe
you tested 277 recipes in less than six weeks! Working with you was
so easy (and delicious!). Thanks to the kids, who pitched in, cooking,
timing, tasting and even delivering the hot food to my door. Devorah
and Motty, thank you for taste testing everything and anything, anytime,
day or night: what a strain!

Then came the writing and recipe editing ...
Karen, I hit the jackpot when I got you as my mother-in-law. This book
would never, ever have happened without your help. You were there
for me, riding the emotional roller coaster of setbacks and successes
with such genuine enthusiasm, interest and excitement. Saying "thank
you" doesn't do you justice. Thanks to Warren and Carly, for sharing
you and tolerating this monstrous project with a smile. And to Bob,
for being considerate of all the time and devotion mom-in-law gave to
this book.

Charlotte, in addition to your talent, wit, humor and vast knowledge,
your sensitivity, warmth and dedication made this book what it is.
Monet, how is it that you are able to help me with everything in life?
Just when I thought all was lost, you pulled a recipe editor out of your
hat – well, out of Evelyn's hat – but you know what I mean. (Yes, Mor-
dechai, both you and the JEC along with Rabbi Lawrence and Anita have
had a tremendous impact on my life. Thanks to you all, too!) Evelyn,
you stepped in quickly and graciously with the most amazing referral
ever. (See the hat above!) Sylvia, the level of expertise you brought to
this project was invaluable. Thank you for extending yourself above
and beyond what was expected and initially requested.

Legal expertise, plus!

Morse, this is a thank you to my lawyer, not my uncle, though no lawyer ever took such warm interest in his client. And thanks to your wonderful wife, my Aunt Judi, for opening your house to us for my first Shabbos with Nachum and ever since.

Next came the photography and design …

Mia, I Group, you found the talented people who knew exactly how to make my cookbook dream come true. Jerry, your pictures are exquisite and your personality a pleasure. Kristen and Lisa, your great style helped make this book beautiful. Kris and Heather, true design talents, you understood, expanded upon and realized my vision. Gina, a real artist, your calligraphy elevated this book. Brian, you're a chef and stylist extraordinaire. Thanks also to Laurie and Alice for your hard work, recipe tweaks and awesome notes.

Then I met the generous folks whose support helped actualize my vision – and whose contributions really took this book to the next level.

A special thank you to some "super" guys …

Mr. Garber and Yaakov, Supersol of Lawrence, NYC, New Rochelle and Scarsdale, New York. Mr. Garber, you believed in me when this project was totally unproven. For that I thank you profusely. Many thanks, as well, to the wonderful managers of the fish, meat, produce and grocery departments (Dave, Levi, Steven and John, respectively) for taking time out of your busy days to graciously entertain all my questions. Ernie and Josh, Hagafen Cellars, it was an honor for me to partner with such a prestigious wine company. Your interview and knowledgeable wine suggestions added elegance, value and helpful information to this book. Izzet and Christophe, Osem, USA, I thank you for taking part in the book and allowing me to share the secrets of Osem seasonings with everyone. Magda and Pamela, PJ Sterling, your store in Cedarhurst, New York, has the most gorgeous silver I have ever seen. I am so thankful to you for lending your exquisite pieces for our photo shoot. Debbie and Shira, Amici, I always walk by your store in Cedarhurst, New York, wishing I had registered there. Luckily, I was able to indulge myself with your stunning collection during the book's photo shoot. Thank you for being so generous. Joe DiMauro, Mt. Kisco Seafood, (Westchester County, NY) thanks for letting us snap shots of your super fresh and gorgeous fish.

BEFORE THE BOOK

Mom, you inspired me to write; I just finished my book first. You are the most unselfish and giving person I have ever encountered. You love so unconditionally and so much, always giving everyone the benefit of the doubt (not to mention second, third and hundredth chances). You are the most remarkable optimist I have ever known. Things always *do* work out; I believe it when you say it. I love you. Dad, you always believed in my success and encouraged me to keep fighting for myself and my dreams. You did everything possible to ensure that I had every opportunity. Thank you. Most important, (despite your tough-as-nails style!) I know you have a big, warm, mushy heart and I love you! My sister, Shoshana, being your sister has been quite an emotional, ever-changing, and rewarding ride. As our relationship changes and evolves, please know that my love is constant. Thanks for everything – including first-run testing of the desserts in this book! Uputzi and Poppy, my two grandfathers, two great chefs from the old country. You have always brought the family together with your delicious meals. I love you both.

Grandma Martha, the matriarch of the Geller family, you are the quintessential grandmother and a great role model, with the warmest, most delightful hug in the world. Judy, you are one of the closest links I have to my father-in-law and I am so thankful that you are open with your memories of this great man. You and Marty have welcomed us into your home and life unconditionally. Many thanks, too, for being on the other end of my SOS cooking calls! Chanie, Abbie and Debbie, you are awesome, inspiring, amazing-in-the-kitchen, incredible moms, wives and sisters-in-law. Thanks for including me, embracing me, helping me (and I'm not just talking about in the kitchen). Brothers-in-law Greg, Eric and Adam: You guys are great also. You know, because behind every great woman there has to be a great man, right?

David, Rachel, Paul and Miriam, thank you for welcoming me into this family with open arms. P&M I'll never forget the b-day cake, and a "thanx in advance" for making sure this book sells like hot tamales in Texas. D&R a special thanks for a beautiful Sheva Brachos and for storing everything under the sun for us – including our precious wine.

Our Rebbi ... Rabbi Greenberg, If there's a better rebbi, a better man, we haven't found him. And thank G-d we have you and your unerring capacity to guide us.

Rabbi Young and Rebbetzin Judy, you sealed the deal, hosted the party and were with me to celebrate and give meaning to every step of my engagement and marriage. Yaffa, you introduced me to Nachum and for that no thanks or repayment will ever be sufficient.

CNN: Lori, a true talent relations guru. You gave me my first big break and I will never forget it. I learned so much from you and always dreamed of one day thanking you, Bonnie and Sam with an Emmy in my hand, but I figured this is better because it will last forever. Scott, you went out on a limb with an unproven novice and gave me my first producing opportunities – the kind that seasoned journalists dream of. Rachel, a friend, a roomie, a guide. I was so scared to leave you and CNN but you were there to support me through the changes and transitions, in work and in life.

HBO: Naomi, you brought me to HBO and opened doors for me toward a career I never expected. Cami, my mentor. Not just a boss but a friend. You fought for me always as a woman, as an employee and as an individual. I've become the producer I am today because of you. Rob, thanks for believing in me and always taking such a warm personal interest in my life. Sue, your fighting spirit, drive,

determination, and success have been such an inspiration to me. I appreciate all the opportunities and special accommodations you made for me. Chris, a great Creative Director, you gave me creative freedom and were always so nice. Spencer, I have such respect for you and the ship you run so well. The HBO marketing team is truly the best in the industry and it is an honor to be a part of it!

Thanks to all of the publications and people who gave me a chance, believed in my book, my story and my writing, edited me wonderfully, published my articles, and gave me local, national, and international recognition. 5 Towns Jewish Times (Larry) Atlanta Jewish Life (Binyomin), Mother's Helper Magazine (Zeesy), The Jewish Press (Jason and Sheila), www.thejewishwoman.org/www.chabad.org (Sara Esther).

This section was originally long enough to be its very own book. I was thinking it could be shrink-wrapped together with the cookbook and sold as a twofer .... Alas, it turned out that wasn't an option. So for all the details I forgot to mention and to all those I may have erroneously left off this list, thank you, *todah raba* and a *groyse dank* for helping to make this dream possible!

Notes

Notes